CARIBOU PUBLIC LIBRARY

BEACHCOMBING AND BEACHCRAFTING

by Anne Wescott Dodd

Edited by Julius M. Wilensky

All photos by Nancy Lemay
All line drawings by Don Johnson

Copyright © *by* **Anne Wescott Dodd**
published by **Wescott Cove Publishing Company**
P.O. Box 130, Stamford, CT 06904

All Rights Reserved

No part of this book may be reproduced in any form
without written permission of the publisher

1st Edition — 1989

Library of Congress Card No. 89-50754
ISBN No. 0-918752-10-8
SAN No. 210-5810

Dedication

For
Kristen, Cori, and Casey
Eric and Marcus
with love

ACKNOWLEDGEMENTS

Many people contributed to this book in a variety of ways—from working to get suitable photos to digging Florida sand in the rain and transporting it to Maine for one of my tables. I am grateful to Claude Bonang and Jon Ross for allowing me to include their crafts; Don Johnson for the line drawings; Nancy Lemay for the black and white photography; Patricia MacRitchie, Frank Brockman, Lois Berge, Glenn Burris, Kate Anderson, Archie H. Wescott, and Felicia Ferrara Wescott for their ideas and other contributions; Juluis Wilensky for believing in the book enough to publish it; and especially Jim Dodd for not only encouraging me when I wanted to quit but also for helping me clean up numerous beaches when he'd much rather have been sailing.

TABLE OF CONTENTS

EDITOR'S PREFACE

Anne Wescott Dodd is an educator who has taught education classes at Bates College and Colby College and basic reading and writing courses at the University of Maine at Augusta. She has written four books in her field of work. Anne recently won an award from the Maine Council for English Language Arts for "significant contribution to education." Along the way, she has become an inveterate beachcomber, and has combed beaches in her travels in many parts of the world.

I share her love of beaches and have greatly enjoyed picking up everything from shells to notes in bottles (I always answer them!). Our porch has a family of 13 horseshoe crabs and we have buckets of small shells and shelves with large ones, driftwood, pretty rocks, etc. I keep bringing more back from my cruises, but it doesn't get too far out of hand because we keep giving this stuff away.

Anne brings home the fruits of her beachcombing also, but she goes me one better. She's learned how to make exquisite handicrafts using stuff she finds on beaches.

When Anne came to us with her idea for this book, we knew that it needed graphics to help people understand "how-to." Besides Nancy Lemay's photos of finished work and work in process, we enlisted the aid of Don Johnson to make excellent line drawings. Yes, this is the same Don Johnson who wrote our best-selling two-volume cruising guides to Maine. Don is a boat builder, ocean-crossing and cruising sailor, with a background in zoology, who also worked for years as a commercial artist. He made line drawings of shells for this book—the best we've ever seen.

Although Anne lives in Brunswick, Maine and Don lives near Eastport, they worked 3000 miles apart. Don sailed his boat to the Azores, then to Dublin last year, and made these drawings during the year he lived there.

Don worked from actual specimens made available to him by the curator of the Shells Department in Dublin's excellent Natural History Museum (part of the National Museum of Ireland). They generously provided Don with office space and produced every shell that we needed from their extensive collection, including many not available for public viewing. We are deeply indebted to: Dr. Colm D. O'Riordan, Keeper of the Natural History Museum; Mr. J.M.C. Holmes, Assistant Keeper; and Mr. Pat O'Sullivan, Senior Technician.

However, as you will see, this is not just another shell book. We are proud to present Anne's work to you, knowing that she and her friends speak from practical hands-on experience. She wants you to enjoy making things the way that she has, and shares her knowledge generously. You can't say you don't have time. Anne is an educator, homemaker, author, and beachcomber extraordinaire, and look what she has made!

PART I: BEACHCOMBING

INTRODUCTION

Do you know that . . .

you can use broken glass (beach glass) or shells to make unusual and incredibly attractive lamps?

a beachcomber's display table is practical for dining?

beachcombing can provide profits as well as pleasure?

fresh water driftwood is whiter and more attractive than its salt water cousin and some "driftwood" can even be found in fields?

the sand dollar contains the gospel of Christ on its shell?

starfish will dry perky, rather than flat, when baked in an oven?

Who can ignore the invitation of a deserted shoreline? Who can resist picking up a shell or two, an unusual rock, or a silver piece of weathered wood as they walk along the beach?

If you're a compulsive beachcomber, you probably already have a collection of shells or beach glass that's taking up space in your home. Throwing out these treasures would be like erasing the nostalgic memories of restful hours by the sea.

You'll discover that you can use just about anything—shells, rocks, broken glass, and washed-up fishing gear—to make many unusual and decorative items for fun or to sell. You can make crafts ranging from large objects, such as tables and lamps, to smaller ones: jewelry, mobiles, candleholders, suncatchers, and paperweights. This book will show you more than 100 ways to utilize the materials that you have collected along the shore. You can make these items and others to decorate your home inside and to landscape outside.

A little patience rather than any special skill is all that you need to make any of the decorative objects described. Spend a rainy summer afternoon or a long winter evening transforming your beachcombing collection into unique sea crafts to delight your family and friends. You'll be pleased with the results and the compliments you'll receive on your talent and creativity.

Welcome to beachcombing and beachcrafting. Have fun!

CHAPTER 1

BEGINNING TIPS FOR BETTER BEACHCOMBING

Whether you're just going to the seashore for a week's vacation or you're lucky enough to live there year-round, beachcombing is a great way to explore an open stretch of sand or a more secluded spot hidden along a twisting, rocky coastline. You can escape the routine hassles and bustle, breathe deeply in the fresh salt air, and exercise effortlessly as you walk along the beach, hunting for not-so-buried treasures. A few hours later you'll feel like a new person. Like many others, you may become a compulsive beachcomber.

Beachcombing requires no special talent although a strong back will come in handy if you covet a large piece of driftwood. Just stroll along the beach, picking up any shell or rock that looks interesting or unusual. Bring along a sturdy bag to collect your gatherings and tote them home. Once your collection at home becomes so large that you run out of storage space, you may have the urge to dump it and begin again. Instead, consider using your carefully selected treasures in crafts. Once you begin crafting, your beachcombing will have another purpose, easier to justify to skeptical friends. And you won't have to fell so guilty about all the things you left undone to go beachcombing. You'll find directions for making many crafts later in this book. Here are a few suggestions for more productive beachcombing.

You don't have to go very far from any city or town near the coast to find a good spot to beachcomb. While beachcombing can be done on people-filled beaches, the best treasures wait to be discovered in the lonelier, less-traveled places where shouts and laughter are replaced by seagulls' screeching, and waves lapping along the shore. Because there are many thousands of miles of coastlines in the world, including many islands, large and small, you'll never run out of new places to go.

Each small area of almost any coast seems to have its own specialty. On one stretch of sand you can find many bits of sea-worn glass. You may not think there's any beach glass on the beaches you visit, but that may be because you haven't looked. I found the small beach at Lahaina on Maui, Hawaii, loaded with beautiful pieces no one else had even noticed, including my friend who lived there. She had never even thought about collecting beach glass until I showed her what could be done with it. On another beach, driftwood seems to be everywhere. You'll know the sea birds have been eating well when you find the spots where they routinely drop their cleaned-out shells. Spend a few minutes looking around in any location and you'll soon see what special treasures you can find there.

Because the best places to beachcomb are the out-of-the-way places where most people don't usually go, you should find a public right-of-way to gain access to the beach. It's not good form to walk across private property without the owner's permission, but the property line in most places extends only to the high tide line. Use a public ramp, dock, or right-of-way to get to the water, continue walking along the beach in either direction and you'll soon be in a less-traveled area. Out of respect for the preservation of the natural environment, never pick or dig up plants, such as sea oats or sea grass, along the shore. They are needed to protect the beach from erosion, and in most places it's also against the law.

If you can borrow or rent a boat, consider going to a small coastal island if there are any in your area. Like the mainland, stretches of island coastline also have their own specialties for beachcombers. Some islands are uninhabited. Here you will probably find shells, rocks, or driftwood. If your interest is beach glass, however, you need to choose an island where people now live or formerly lived. Beach glass comes from trash that has been carelessly dumped. The best pieces are those that are worn so smooth they look like pieces of penny candy. They get this way from being tossed around for many years by storms and tides. Because fewer people go to the islands than to mainland beaches, you'll find that island beachcombing is more productive. This doesn't apply to larger densely populated islands.

If you can, make time to beachcomb in the spring, early in the summer, and just after a storm. Every time the weather drives the ocean wild, more debris is strewn along the shore. If you are a serious beachcomber, you'll want to get to your favorite spots before someone else picks them clean of all the best shells, driftwood, beach glass, flotsam (ship wreckage) and jetsam (material thrown overboard and later washed ashore).

Check the tides before you go. The best beachcombing is at low or middle tide. You'll have more beach to explore then and you won't run the risk of having to walk on someone else's property above the high tide line. Be careful, however, when the tide is on its way in. In some places it's easy to find yourself stranded on a sandbar which connects to the mainland only when the tide is at its lowest. In others, you may find that instead of walking along a sandy stretch of beach the way you came, the only way back is over an obstacle course of slippery, steep rocks. Don't get so involved in your search that you neglect to notice what the sea is doing.

Learn where to look for certain items. Tide pools, those little pockets of water left in the crevices of rocks after the tide goes out, often harbor starfish, tiny crabs, and other small creatures. Starfish may also be found hiding under the wet seaweed in cracks in the rocks. Scuba divers can obtain large starfish lying on the bottom offshore. The largest starfish my editor has ever seen were on a sandy bottom in 20-foot depths off the west shore of Union Island in St. Vincent's Grenadines. If you're interested in finding pieces of fishnet or cork floats, you'll need to explore areas where fishing boats regularly work the waters. These are becoming very scarce today because fishermen now use styrofoam floats on their nets. Beach glass is plentiful only where bottles were thrown away at some time in the past, but the beach should now look quite clean. If the area looks as if it is currently being used as a dump site, you will find only jagged pieces of broken glass, not the well-polished treasures you seek.

Don't always look for driftwood just at the water's edge. You can do some "beachcombing" even if you're far from the sea! Driftwood comes in two varieties. Salt water driftwood is not as white and smooth as fresh water driftwood known as "dri-ki." The name may be short for "dry kindling." Besides looking along the beach for driftwood, you may also want to look in fields. The wood is bleached whiter by the sun when it is not kept wet by salt water. Beautiful pieces of dri-ki are especially plentiful in areas where trees were cleared to build roads, dams, or other construction projects. Driftwood is probably a misnomer in this case, but if you keep your eyes open, you may spot a special piece of weathered wood as you drive along country roads. *Editor's Note: Some of the best "driftwood" I've seen has been in the deserts of west Texas, New Mexico, Arizona, Nevada, Utah, Southern California and the Baja California Peninsula. Tourist handicraft shops in all these places sell "driftwood" items.*

Not everything you may want from beachcombing is free. Such treasures as lobster or crab traps and buoys are not only hard to find, but since they are part of the fisherman's tools of the trade, they are also not available for the taking even when you find them washed up on the shore. Broken pieces of traps and buoys aren't of any use to fishermen, but may be useful to you in making some crafts. If you want a weathered lobster trap in good condition to make a table, or a buoy to fashion into a lamp, your best bet is to make a deal with a lobsterman. You'll see places along some coastal roads which sell these items to tourists, but you'll have more fun—and a better story to tell—by making friends with a fisherman. Some fisherman will also be glad to give you starfish, sea urchins, and the like which get picked up in their nets along with fish.

Although occasionally you will find bits and pieces of fishnet along the shore, you will have to purchase the net if you want a large quantity for curtains or decoration. Use the yellow pages or ask a fisherman where you can buy fishnet in the color and mesh size you desire. The net that comes in patio decorating kits is priced quite high for the amount you get. Other than the items which the fishermen use in their work, whatever else you want is yours for the taking.

Beachcombing is fun and relaxing. You'll be surprised at what you'll be able to find. Chapter Two describes some of these possibilities. If you're a scuba diver, you can go beyond the beach and also look for treasures underwater.

If you don't have a chance to do your own shell collecting because you can't get to a beach but would still like to make some crafts, you can purchase shells. Check your local craft store or look for mail order ads in the classified sections of general interest magazines. The Shell Factory in Fort Myers, Florida, is primarily a retail store with shells of every size, shape, and description for sale. If all else fails, write to the Shell Factory and ask if you can order shells by mail. Shell stores are scattered over Cape Cod and other resort areas. Unfortunately beach glass is not something you can buy, but you can make your own by tumbling some broken glass in a rock polisher. I've never tried making artificial beach glass—it seemed like cheating—but I must admit I've thought about it several times to get more pieces of red glass. Red beach glass is very rare.

A quahog shell makes an attractive soap dish

CHAPTER TWO

TREASURES TO HUNT BY THE SEA

Many types of shells, sea creatures, rocks, driftwood, beach glass or sea glass, and other remnants of sea and land can be found along the coast and used for beachcrafting. Following are some of the things you can enjoy discovering on the beach and later use to make all kinds of beautiful and practical items.

You can make crafts without knowing what to call your raw materials. If you're interested in identifying what you pick up, however, you'll find a mini-guide to shells and sea animals in Chapter Three. Complete directions for making the crafts appear later in this book.

You'll find many creatures you probably don't want—beach and sand fleas, sea anemones and jelly fish, to name a few—but pick up anything that looks interesting to you. Once you begin beachcrafting, you'll have no trouble finding a use for it later.

SHELLS

Shells, which come from one of the largest and oldest groups of animals called mollusks, have been used by people throughout history in many ways. In the Middle Ages pilgrims wore scallop shells on their hats to show that they had crossed the sea to the Holy Land—that's why these shells are sometimes called "pilgrim shells." The North American Indians made small polished beads from shells to use as money (wampum) and jewelry. In the Philippines and elsewhere shells have been substituted for glass in windows.

Oyster shells are widely used today for building roads and driveways, especially in Bermuda. When they are flattened down by traffic, they make an excellent surface for driving. Oyster shells also grace driveways in Norwalk, Connecticut, and in Chesapeake Bay towns. These shells have been called "the poor man's bluestone."

Another use for shells recently brought protests from animal rights activists in Wales who tried to stop villagers in Swansea from holding a cockle-tossing contest as part of a village fair. The Royal Society for the Prevention of Cruelty to Animals said that putting handfuls of cockles into socks and throwing them across a field was cruel and frivolous.

Mollusks are divided into five classes—amphineura, pelecypoda, gastropoda, scaphoda, and cephalopoda—but beachcombers will discover that the shells they find come mainly from the second and third classes because these species are the most numerous.

Amphineura

Chitons are one example of the AMPHINEURA class and the only animals in this class which have shells. Chiton shells are made up of eight plates held together by a band or girdle, giving them the appearance of being dressed in knight's armor. Chitons all live in the sea. See Chapter Three for an illustration of one type.

Pelecypoda

PELECYPODS are more commonly known as bivalves because their shells come in two parts which are held together by a hinge. This class includes the largest of all shells, the **Tridacna** clam of the South Pacific which may be over three feet long, two feet high, and weigh more than five hundred pounds. Bivalves live in both salt and fresh water. Clams are a good example of ocean bivalves because different varieties can be found on both the Atlantic and Pacific coasts. In California you'll find **Pismo clams** in the south and **Pacific littlenecks** in the north. Clams in New York or Maryland are **little necks** or **cherrystones**. All of these are hard shell clams.

In New England it is the **steamer** or long neck, a soft-shell clam, which is most numerous. Steamers live buried in mud flats, but you will find empty shells washed up on shore nearly everywhere. Steamer clam shells are whitish gray and are usually about 3-4 inches long. You may discover a clam shaped like the old straight-edge razor: the **razor clam**, also known as a jackknife clam, grows to 6 or 7 inches long.

Quahogs (pronounced CO-hogs) or hard-shell clams are rounder, fatter, and larger than soft-shell clams. Empty quahog shells are much deeper and heavier than their slimmer clam cousins and may be used as ashtrays, cooking "dishes" for stuffed seafood recipes, candleholders, or soap dishes. Shells of larger bivalves, such as **abalones** in California, make attractive containers for small plants.

Clams and quahogs, like several other bivalves, are good to eat. If you're in the right area for steamer clams, you can find out why they're called steamers by digging some to bring home for dinner. Make sure the area is open to clam digging. Some areas are posted because of red tide or other pollution, and you may need a license to dig any at all or more than a small number for your personal consumption.

The clams you've dug will clean themselves in a few hours if you put them in a pail filled with sea water and sprinkle corn meal on top of the water. Then when you are ready to cook the clams, steam them in a small amount of sea or salted water in a large kettle until the shells open. Save the broth. Serve the clams in their shells with cups of broth and melted butter. If you've never eaten steamed clams before, don't worry: they taste better than they look! Take the clam from the shell, strip the black cover from its neck, dip it first in broth and then in butter, and pop it in your mouth. Some people prefer not to eat the black neck, often referred to as the "head," so they use it to hold the clam as they dip, then discard it after they bite off the rest.

Many people like to eat clams or quahogs raw, dipped in cocktail sauce or horseradish, as hors d'oeuvres. If you want to try quahogs this way, be sure to use only the small ones. The big ones are tough! Quahogs can also be steamed like clams. Use leftover clams or quahogs to make a New England clam chowder. See the section entitled "Incredible Edibles" in Chapter 12 for a delicious real Down East recipe.

Mussels, bivalves which usually live in dense colonies attached to rocks or wharf pilings, are also good for crafting and eating. The **Atlantic ribbed mussels** grow to 2–4 inches while the **blue edible mussels** are somewhat smaller, about 1–3 inches.

Other kinds of mussels, such as the **Variable Mussel** of Africa and the Mediterranean, can be found in other parts of the world. For most crafts, you will probably want to collect only the empty shells which are strewn across the beach. Some of these dark blue mussel shells have been bleached by the sun to light shades of lavender. You may find really tiny mussel shells as small as ¼ to ½ inch long as well as sea-polished pieces which look like chips of lavender pearl.

If you're hungry and ambitious, gather living mussels from rocks or pilings and take them home for a seafood treat. They can be cooked in wine sauce (a recipe appears in Chapter 12.) or simply steamed like clams and eaten directly from the shell after being dipped in broth and melted butter. Save the prettiest shells for your crafts, perhaps leaving them outside for a while to bleach in the sun. Use the others along with clam and quahog shells to begin a walkway by stomping on the shells to crunch them into chunks like gravel.

Bivalves can also be quite delicate. **Slipper shells** are so named because when one is turned upsidedown, the pocket on the underside gives it the look of a scuff-type slipper.

Some bivalves, such as **scallops**, live in moderately deep water, but some do wash up or have been dumped on Mid-Atlantic and New England beaches. Both the **Iceland scallop**, which is reddish brown and ripped, and the **Atlantic (or Deep Sea) scallop**, reddish to pinkish brown, grow to about 4 inches. Smaller scallop shells are everywhere on the shelling beaches in Florida. Bleached by the sun and worn thin as they are tossed by tides, some scallop shells can be very special and exciting to find when you're beachcombing.

Gastropoda

You probably know GASTROPODS as **snails**. Their shell is composed of only one piece; thus, they are also called univalves. Most have coiled shells, but they may be smooth, have long spines, or be covered with ribs or nodules. These shells are very numerous and can be found living everywhere: on land, in fresh water, in the deep sea, and along the shore.

Salt water gastropods vary greatly in size. Very tiny **periwinkles** may be less than a quarter inch while larger snails of three inches or more furnish food for birds who drop the empty shells after eating the meat inside. *Editor's Note: Seagulls take their shellfish high up dropping them on a hard surface to break the shells and get to the meat. Parking lots near shore in New England are littered with broken shells in the winter time when not many people are about.* **Conchs,** such as the one used as a symbol of power in William Golding's well-known novel, *Lord of the Flies,* are also gastropods.

In many areas you will find living creatures in the small shells in tide pools and shallow water, but the bigger creatures live in deeper water and only the empty shells are washed ashore. One large snail variety about the size of a plum, pearly or blue-gray in color, is the **moon snail.** Although you won't find such a large snail in a tide pool, their empty shells are often washed up or dropped by birds on the beach.

If you discover some of the smaller living creatures in water captured in a crevice of the rocks after the tide has gone out, watch them move around. One of them which looks like a snail is really a **hermit crab,** and, when it comes out of its shell, you will see it use its tiny crab claws to move from one place to another. Hermit crabs merely take over empty shells, moving to larger quarters—other vacant shells—as they grow.

Dunce caps, or limpets, are also gastropods although their shells are flatter and more cone-shaped than coiled like other univalves. They are appealing little shells whose name derives from the fact that they look like the old-fashioned cap a student who misbehaved in school had to wear as he sat in the corner on a stool.

You will find small gastropods in a variety of colors: white, gold, yellow, blue-gray, black, and interesting variations caused by their exposure to the sun.

Scaphodopa

SCAPHOPODS are often called tooth shells. They are long shells of one piece shaped like a tube but with openings on both ends. A small group of mollusks, tooth shells are found only in the ocean. It is these shells that the North American Indians used for currency and that one sometimes sees made into necklaces. Tooth shells are not very common beachcombing finds.

Cephalopoda

Because the CEPHALOPODA class of mollusks includes such species as **squid, cuttlefish, and octopus,** you can quickly see why beachcombers won't have much interest in them. Most have very small shells inside their bodies, but one variety, the **nautilus,** builds itself a rather heavy shell to live in. The female **Argonauta,** or **paper nautilus,** constructs a very beautiful thin, fluted shell for storing her eggs. All Cephalopods live in the ocean.

Anatomy of Gastropod

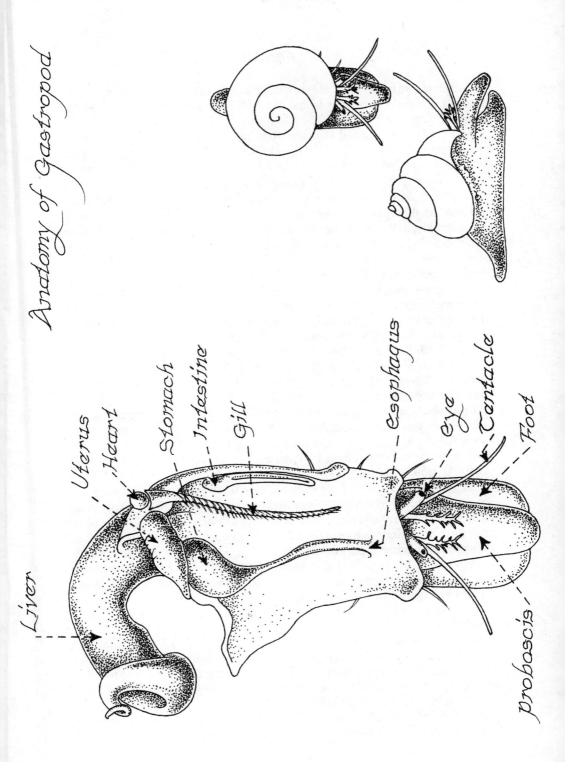

Liver

Uterus
Heart
Stomach
Intestine
Gill

Esophagus

Eye
Tentacle
Foot

Proboscis

SEA CREATURES

Several sea animals also provide the beachcomber with good material for crafts. Here are several you may find. Illustrations of these and others appear in Chapter 3.

Sand Dollars, so named because they resemble the silver dollar coin, are becoming harder to find. When you do spot them, they will punctuate the smooth, wet sand with their round and intricately designed shells. What is washed ashore is only the shell, or test, of the sand dollar. The two types of sand dollars you'll find, the **common** and the **key hole**, are very similar. The key hole sand dollar has five good-sized holes spotted on its upper shell, while the common sand dollar's only holes are tiny ones defining its center. Sand dollars can be found on sandy ocean bottoms all over the world, but look for them only on open ocean beaches because they cannot live in brackish water.

The legend attached to the sand dollar is both quite well known and very interesting. According to the story, you can see the Gospel of Christ when you examine a sand dollar closely. The five holes in the shell represent the four nail holes put through Christ to hang him on the cross as well as a fifth hole made by a Roman's spear. On one side the Easter lily appears with a star, the one the sheperds followed, as its center; on the other, the Christmas poinsettia is etched. And, if the sand dollar is broken open, five white doves which spread good will and peace will be released. You can easily see everything except the doves just by looking at the next sand dollar you find. If you don't want to break your shell to release the five white doves, take my word for it: they are there! Shake the shell and you'll hear them rattle. These five pieces that rattle are really a set of teeth called Aristotle's lantern.

Sea Urchins, half-round creatures with spines poking out on all sides, are fun to find. **North Atlantic sea urchins** have green spines while some **black and white tropical** ones look like little skunks of the sea. The black ones have very sharp spines that can easily pierce your skin, break off inside you, and cause a painful inflammation. Handle them with care. An application of hot lime will dissolve spines that cannot be pulled out with tweezers. Another variety of sea urchin found in the waters of the South Pacific has large tan and white spines about five inches long and three-fourths of an inch in diameter. Their spines are excellent for making wind chimes.

The best sea urchin are those you find intact with all the spines attached. Some are devoid of spines and have been bleached white by the sun. Be careful carrying these porcupine-like sea creatures because their shells are very fragile. If you toss a sea urchin into a bag with other shells, you'll end up with only broken pieces.

Starfish, relatives of the sand dollar and sea urchin, can be found when the tide is low in tide pools or hidden under the wet seaweed in rock crev-

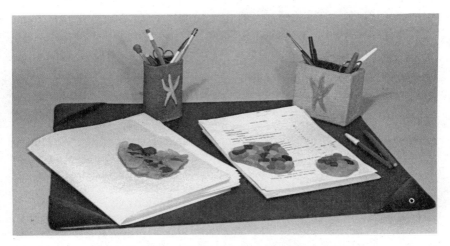

Starfish decorate pencil holders in this beachcrafted set.
Paperweights have beach glass decor

ices. Since they are enemies of the oyster, long ago some Connecticut fishermen used to pay kids fifty cents a bushel to pick them up in the harbor. Starfish which you can find along the shore are small, probably only 2–3 inches, because the larger starfish live in deeper water.

If you want really good-sized starfish, you might find a fisherman who can save you some which come up in his nets or traps, or dive for them in tropical waters, or buy them from a shell shop. Most starfish are rather drab in color, but one South Pacific variety is such a beautiful deep blue/purple that it looks artificial.

Crabs which you find alive on the shore will also be small because, like starfish, the large crabs live in deep water. If you want large crabs, you'll have to befriend a fisherman or visit a seafood store. Some very large **horseshoe crab** shells, however, will be left along the shore admidst the dried seaweed.

Horseshoe crabs are not true crabs; they are more closely related to spiders than crustaceans. Their shells, not surprisingly, are shaped like horse shoes; they have large, rather bulky bodies, and long, thin tails. Because they are so unusual, horse shoe crab shells make great conversation pieces.

Also pick up crab or lobster claws even though they aren't attached to a body. You will find neat ways to use them in your crafts.

ROCKS FOR HOUNDS AS WELL AS WARRIERS

No matter where you live, you can find unusual rocks. You will have many reasons for picking up rocks as you beachcomb: some because they

17

glitter (usually because they are made up in part of mica), others because they have interesting shapes or unusual colors, and still others because they feel so smooth.

Very smooth stones are called "feeling stones" by some people and used in much the same way that Greeks manipulate worry beads. Carry one in your pocket and, when you feel nervous or tense, rub the smooth surface of the stone to calm yourself. According to many, the feeling stone works better than tranquilizers!

Rocks covered all over with barnacles make great samples of the sea shore to carry home. Be careful handling rocks with barnacles. Their tops are razor sharp and can scratch you! True rock hounds can add many varieties from the coast to their collections. If you're interested in rock collecting as a hobby, you can buy a guide which tells you how to identify types of rocks.

Rocks can be free souvenirs of the trips you've taken. Everywhere I've traveled in the world I've brought back small rocks—samples of the honey-colored stone from which most of the buildings in Jerusalem are constructed, volcanic rock from Hawaii, and pink limestone and alabaster from Egypt—which I have labeled and displayed in a glass-topped table. Directions for making such a table appear in Chapter 5.

Consider using rocks by themselves as natural sculptures or combined with driftwood as wall or table art.

Large rocks have other uses. Interesting and unusually shaped rocks can become part of the landscaping around your house or be used to make a rock garden. Volcanic rock formations especially can be very eye-catching both in color and shape. The Chinese depend on rocks along with water, architecture, and plants to make a garden. The rocks always appear in their natural state. The subtle beauty of the gardens comes from the way these four required elements are balanced and combined.

If you want to line a walkway or build a wall with flat rocks, you can find stretches of the shore where the rock has been slivered over time into just the kind of flat, smooth stones you seek. On other parts of the coastline you can find many chunks of granite or other rocks suitable for outlining a flower bed. Large rocks are heavy, and you will have to make several trips if you're collecting enough rocks for projects of this magnitude. Your reward will be the natural beauty of the finished project.

Although coral is a plant, not a rock, when it is dead and dry, it can be used in many of the same ways rocks can be. Small, delicate pieces of softly colored fan coral which looks like frozen lace can add interest to a curio shelf or stand alone as a sculpture in miniature. Coral can also be combined with shells in jewelry and other crafts. It is against the law in most tropical areas to pick living coral, but you'll find many kinds, including fan coral, torn loose by wave action and cast up on the beach.

Sea craft candle holders using driftwood,
shells, beach glass, stones and cork

DRIFTWOOD ON THE BEACH AND IN THE FIELD

As you walk along the shore looking for driftwood, consider how you
might use the silvery wood you see. Flat, weathered pieces of board will
make good signs. Large, unusual driftwood sculptures might become
lamps or plant decorations as well as free-standing works of natural art.
Mobiles require branch-like pieces of varying lengths: the longest one of
the main part of the mobile and several shorter pieces to hang from it.
Even if you aren't sure what you'll be able to do with it, pick up any piece
of driftwood that appeals to you for whatever reason. It won't be difficult
later to find more than one way you can use it.

Don't forget to look for driftwood in fields and other places where trees
may have been cut by man or blown down by storms. Driftwood is really
just weathered wood, and it can "weather" anywhere! "Dri-ki," fresh water (or "fresh air") driftwood, will be silvery white and often more beautiful
than the gray-toned pieces of wood you'll find on salt water shores.

BEACH GLASS: PEOPLE'S TRASH TRANSFORMED

Beach or sea glass, treasures made by nature from people's trash, is as
useful as it is beautiful. Look for well-worn pieces with no sharp edges.

19

The small ones look like gumdrops when they're dry and sparkle like jewels when they're wet. You might miss the very tiny pieces unless you examine a small area very carefully. Sometimes they are so tiny, it's difficult to separate the glass chips from the coarse grains of sand, but it's this size that you need to make some kinds of jewelry. On the other hand, don't overlook large pieces which might be smooth only on one side because they serve as bases for paperweights or suncatchers.

Finding some beach glass is like discovering a bit of history. Some old-fashioned glass turns to beautiful shades of lavender and aqua when it ages. You may recognize the source of some of your beach glass: stoppers from perfume decanters, the ridged surface from the glass shelf of an old refrigerator, the ring left from the top of a soda bottle, or small bits of carnival glass dinnerware. Progress is one reason that red glass is very rare. Automobile tail lights once made from glass are now plastic. As more and more soft drinks come in plastic containers rather than glass bottles and as we work to clean the litter from the beaches, there will be less and less beach glass. In fact, you can justify your search for beach glass by realizing that you're helping to clean up the coastline.

Because many of the pieces of beach glass are small, you'll find that when you're looking for glass, you shouldn't try to look for driftwood and shells at the same time. You need to tune your eyes to see the beach glass. Some colors, green, for example, are easy to spot while others, such as brown and white, although quite plentiful, blend in with the sand and rocks and are difficult to see. Red often looks like brown until you pick the glass up and hold it up to the sun. Don't overlook a piece of red beach glass. It is really a find!

The angle at which you view the beach will determine what you will see. After you've walked along the ocean in one direction, turn around and walk back over the same stretch. You'll undoubtedly find some really special pieces that you missed the first time. When you've found an area where tiny pieces of glass are numerous, stop and carefully examine the sand in very small patches. A place where you thought you saw only one or two good pieces will often yield many more.

Take some care with the glass you have collected. Pieces can be broken just by dumping the contents of your bag on a table. You will be very disappointed to find that you have broken some special pieces by later tossing large, heavy chunks of glass into the bag on top of them. If you do forget, take heart. All is not lost because these chips can be used in jewelry.

COLLECTIBLES FROM THE LOCAL FISHERMAN

The fishing industry provides other washed up treasures which you shouldn't overlook when you're beachcombing. Cork floats and bits of fishnet are useful for decoration by themselves or as part of some other item, such as a lamp or wall hanging. Cork floats also make great candleholders. Broken pieces of lobster or crab traps and buoys can be used in various crafts.

If you want whole traps or buoys or large amounts of fishnet, you will have to purchase them. Traps and buoys in good condition still belong to the fisherman even when they have broken loose and end up with the seaweed and driftwood along the shore.

No fisherman will look kindly upon anyone who touches his equipment. Stories abound along the coast of fishermen who got revenge on those who were foolish enough to mess with traps that didn't belong to them. You won't want to be the subject of one of these gruesome legends! So purchase a used lobster trap and get the barnacle-encrusted, worn look for no extra cost.

You never can tell what else you may find along the shore. Great treasures have been buried at sea when ships went down. Think of the pieces of eight that were just recovered from the *Concepcion*! Of course, finding pieces of real silver washed up on the shore is unlikely, but a piece of red beach glass seems almost as valuable to me. You can also make some really neat things from what others call trash.

Grab your walking shoes and a big bag and head to the shore! Part II of this book will show you what to do with your collection when you bring it home.

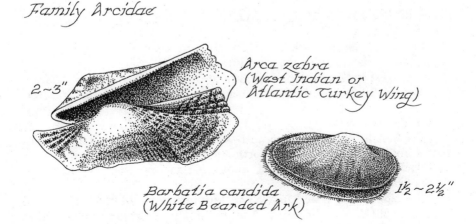

Family Arcidae

2~3"

Arca zebra
(West Indian or
Atlantic Turkey Wing)

Barbatia candida
(White Bearded Ark)

1½ ~ 2½"

21

CHAPTER 3

ILLUSTRATED MINI-GUIDE TO
SHELLS AND SEA ANIMALS

If you're interested in knowing the names of the shells and sea animals you pick up on the beach, or where you are likely to find a particular type, here is a brief guide for many of them. For more complete information, you can refer to one of the books listed in the bibliography.

No attempt is made to describe the colors of shells since many of the shells you'll find on the beach will be bleached by the sun or perhaps discolored by some pollutant. An exception is jingle shells which are brilliant shades of orange and yellow with pearlescent white around the edges.

To identify the shells you pick up, look carefully at their shapes and match them to the illustrations drawn here. You can figure out what general category a shell fits even if the specific variety you have picked up is not included here.

If you collect shells rather than use them to make crafts, you'll want to know their scientific names. Shell crafters will care less about this information. The shells described below are listed by their common names, but the scientific names are included in the line drawings.

MULLUSKS

Chitons (Amphineura)

The Common **West Indian Chiton**, about 2–3 inches, can be found in the Caribbean, Florida, the West Indies, and Bermuda. Other varieties of chitons can be found on shores elsewhere.

Bivalves (Pelecypoda)
ARK SHELLS

The **White Bearded Ark**, about 1½–2½ inches, can be found on the Atlantic Ocean shores from the Carolinas to Brazil.

The **West Indian Turkey Wing**, about 2–3 inches, is also an Atlantic shell which can be found from the Carolinas to the West Indies and Bermuda.

MUSSELS

The **Blue Edible Mussel**, about 1–3 inches, lives in the Atlantic Ocean waters both of Europe and of North America.

The **Atlantic Ribbed Mussel**, about 2–4 inches, is native to ocean shores from Canada to Texas.

The **Non-boring Date Mussel**, chestnut brown in color, about 1 to 1½ inches, is found from Oregon to Sonora, Mexico, in colonies attached to wharf pilings and breakwaters.

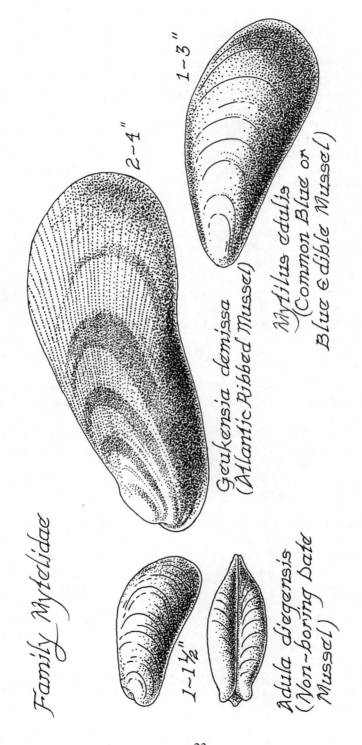

Family Mytelidae

2~4"

1~3"

Geukensia demissa
(Atlantic Ribbed Mussel)

Mytilus edulis
(Common Blue or
Blue edible Mussel)

1~1½"

Adula diegensis
(Non-boring Date
Mussel)

SCALLOPS

The **Atlantic Deepsea Scallop**, about 5–8 inches inhabits Atlantic waters from Labrador to the Carolinas.

The **Calico Scallop**, 1–2 inches, can be found on East Coast beaches of the United States and in the Caribbean.

The **Atlantic Bay Scallop**, 2–4 inches, lives in shallow waters of the Eastern United States.

Lion's Paw, about 3–6 inches, can be found in Atlantic waters from the Southern United States to Brazil and in the Caribbean.

The **Japanese Baking Scallop**, about 2½–3½ inches, is a Pacific variety and can be found from Japan to the South Pacific islands of New Caledonia and Tonga.

JINGLE SHELLS

The **Common Jingle Shells**, about 1–2 inches, are common in the Atlantic from Massachusetts to Brazil.

The **Saddle or Pacific Jingle Shells**, about 3 inches and up, live in the Western Pacific Ocean.

OYSTERS

The **Pacific Thorny Oyster** grows up to 5 inches and lives in the Gulf of California and south to Panama.

The **Kitten's Paw**, about 1 inch, can be found in warmer waters of both the Atlantic and Pacific Oceans.

The **Eastern or Virginia Oyster**, about 2–6 inches, lives on the Atlantic coast.

The **Pacific Pearl Oyster**, about 1½–3 inches, lives in the warmer waters of the Pacific and is similar to the **Atlantic Pearl Oyster** which is not illustrated here.

The **Atlantic Wing Oyster**, about 3 inches, can be found in North American ocean waters. A similar species lives on the other side of the Atlantic from Southern England to the Mediterranean.

The **Sadle Oyster**, 2 to 3 inches, belongs to the same family as the common jingle shell (above).

PEN SHELLS

The **Rude Pen Shell**, from 7 to 22 inches in length, lives on both sides of the Atlantic in deeper, warmer waters.

The **Amber Pen Shell**, from 4 to 9 inches, also lives in deeper, warmer waters of both sides of the Atlantic Ocean. Some giant sized Pen Shells are found in the South Pacific. These can be 12 to 18 inches.

CHESTNUT or ASTARTE CLAM

This clam, about 1–2 inches, lives in almost all of the cold water in the Northern Hemisphere: in Europe, in North America as far south as Massachusetts, and in Asia south to Northern Japan.

LUCINA SHELLS

The **Pacific Tiger Lucina**, about 5 inches, can be found in the tropical waters of the Pacific Ocean.

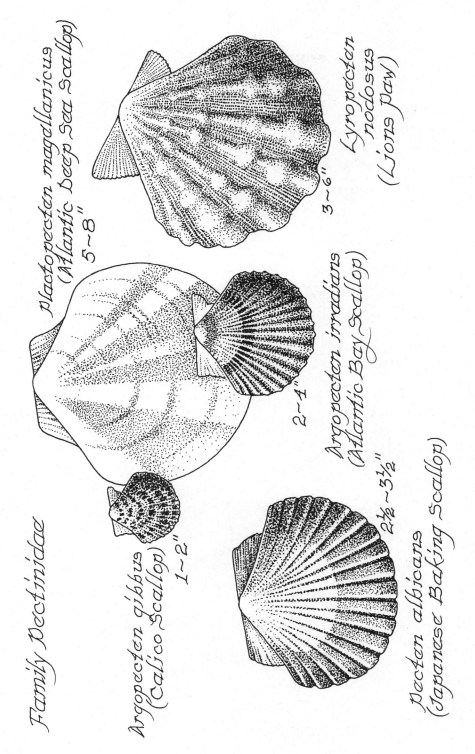

Family Pectinidae

Placopecten magellanicus
(Atlantic Deep Sea Scallop)
5~8"

Lyropecten nodosus
(Lions Paw)
3~6"

Argopecten gibbus
(Calico Scallop)
1~2"

Argopecten irradians
(Atlantic Bay Scallop)
2~4"

Pecten albicans
(Japanese Baking Scallop)
2½~3½"

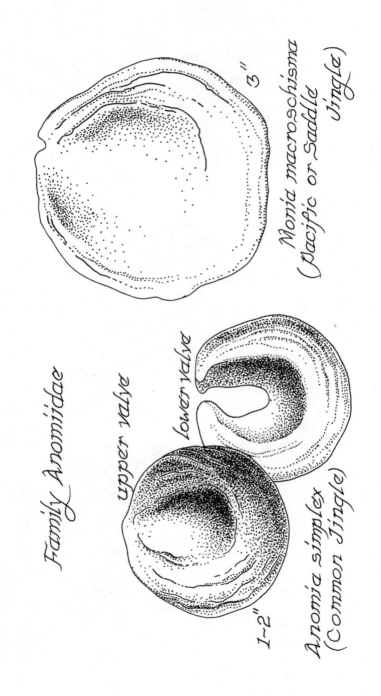

Family Anomiidae

upper valve

lower valve

Monia macroschisma
(Pacific or Saddle
Jingle)

3"

Anomia simplex
(Common Jingle)

1-2"

26

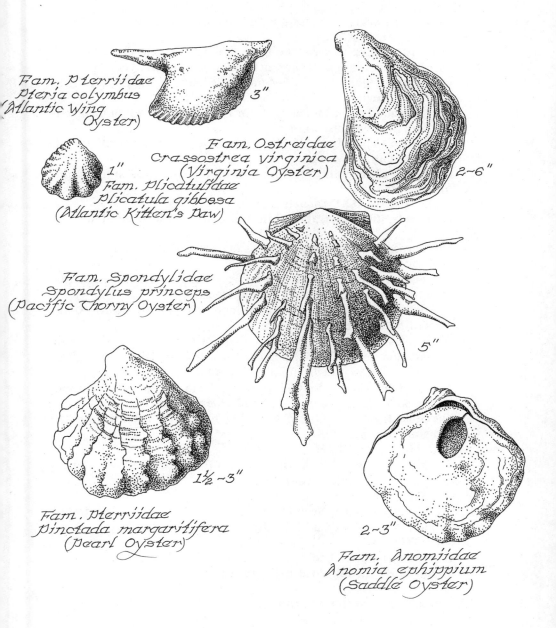

Fam. Pteriidae
Pteria colymbus
(Atlantic Wing
Oyster)   3"

Fam. Ostreidae
Crassostrea virginica
(Virginia Oyster)

1"

Fam. Plicatulidae
Plicatula gibbosa
(Atlantic Kitten's Paw)

2~6"

Fam. Spondylidae
Spondylus princeps
(Pacific Thorny Oyster)

5"

Fam. Pteriidae
Pinctada margaritifera
(Pearl Oyster)   1½~3"

2~3"

Fam. Anomiidae
Anomia ephippium
(Saddle Oyster)

The **Florida Lucina**, about 1½ inches, is native to the shores of Florida and the Caribbean.

COCKLE or HEART SHELLS

The **Prickly Cockle**, about 2 inches, can be found on Atlantic seashores from North Carolina to Florida and the West Indies.

The **Heart Cockle**, 3 inches, lives in tropical waters of the Pacific.

HARD SHELL CLAMS

The **Littleneck or Cherrystone Clam**, about 3–5 inches, lives on the Middle Atlantic coastlines of the Eastern United States.

The **Northern Quahog**, from 2–4 inches, is found in the Eastern United States, New England.

The **Common Pacific Littleneck**, from 1½–2 inches, lives on the Pacific coast from San Francisco north.

The **Calico Clam**, about 1½–2½ inches, is found in the Southern Atlantic and the Gulf of Mexico.

The **Pismo Clam**, about 5 inches, lives on the Pacific coast from mid-California south.

TELLIN AND MACOMA SHELLS

The **Candy Stick Tellin**, about 1 inch, is native to Florida and the Caribbean.

The **Carpenter's Tellin**, which is less than one inch, lives in the warm waters of the Pacific coast.

The **Sunrise Tellin**, about 2 to 4 inches, is found along the Atlantic shoreline from South Carolina to South America.

The **Balthic Macoma**, about ½ to 1½ inches, lives in the North Atlantic waters of both America and Europe.

RAZOR CLAMS

The **Atlantic Razor Clam**, which can grow to 10 inches in length, can be found along the Atlantic from Labrador to the Carolinas.

The **Jackknife Clam**, about 5 inches, can be found along the European Atlantic south to Africa and in the Mediterranean.

The **Stout Tagelus**, about 2 to 3½ inches, lives in the Atlantic from the Carolinas to the Caribbean.

ATLANTIC SURF CLAM

This clam grows to 7 inches and lives in the warm shallow waters of the Atlantic and the Gulf of Mexico.

SOFT SHELL CLAMS

The **Steamer or Long Neck Clam**, about 1 to 6 inches, can be found both in the North Atlantic and Pacific.

ANGEL WINGS

Angel Wings, about 4 to 7 inches, can be found in Atlantic waters from Massachusetts south to Brazil and the Caribbean.

Univalves/Sea Snails (Gastropods)

LIMPETS

The **Atlantic Plate Limpet**, 1 to 1½ inches, is a New England Shell.

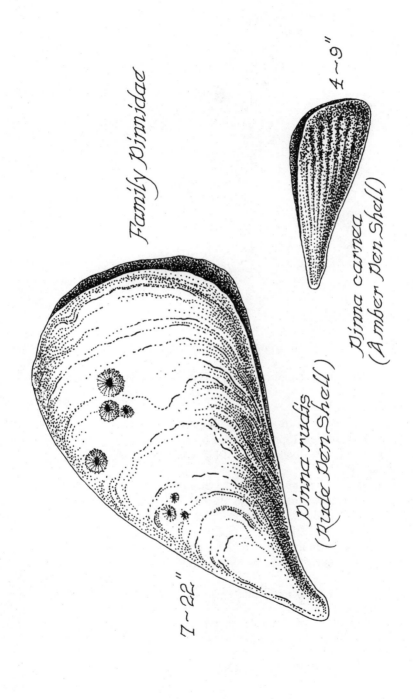

Family Pinnidae

7 ~ 22"

Pinna rudis
(Rude Pen Shell)

4 ~ 9"

Pinna carnea
(Amber Pen Shell)

Family Astartidae

Astarte borealis
(Boreal or Chestnut Astarte)

The **Giant Keyhole Limpet**, 2½ to 5 inches, can be found in California.

The **Barbados Keyhole Limpet**, about 1 inch, lives in Florida and the West Indies.

TOP SHELLS

The **Strawberry Top**, about 1 inch, is an Indian Ocean shell.

The **West Indian Top Shell**, about 3 inches, has a heavy operculum, is greenish-black, and lives on subtidal rocks in the Caribbean.

ABALONE

The **Green Abalone**, about 7 to 8 inches, can be found in California from Point Conception south to Baja.

The **Red Abalone**, about 10 to 12 inches, lives along the Atlantic from Canada south to Virginia.

The **Atlantic Shark Eye**, 1 to 2½ inches, is an Atlantic shell which can be found from Massachusetts to the Gulf shores of Texas.

COWRIES

The **Atlantic Gray and Yellow Cowries**, about 1 inch, can be found in Florida and the Caribbean.

The **Tiger Cowrie**, from 2½ to 4½ inches, lives in the Indian and Pacific Oceans, but there are many versions of this species in many sizes in many places.

HELMET SHELLS AND CONCHS

The **Queen Helmet**, about 4 to 9 inches lives along the Atlantic coast from the Carolinas south to Florida and the Caribbean.

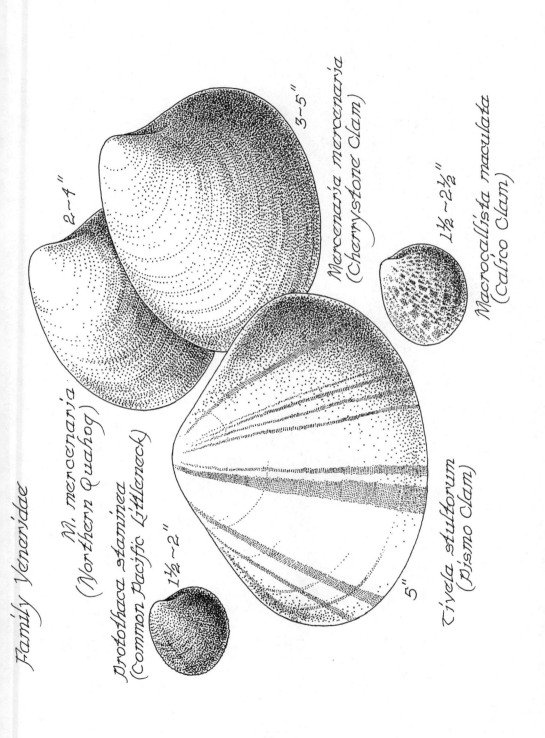

Family Veneridae

M. mercenaria
(Northern Quahog)

Protothaca staminea
(Common Pacific Littleneck)

2~4"

3~5"

Mercenaria mercenaria
(Cherrystone Clam)

Macrocallista maculata
(Calico Clam)

1½~2½"

1½~2"

Tivela stultorum
(Pismo Clam)

5"

31

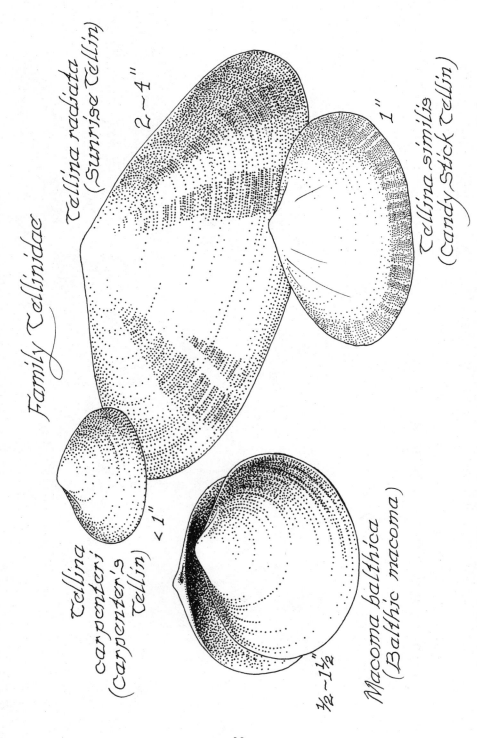

Family Tellinidae

Tellina radiata (Sunrise Tellin)
2~4"

Tellina similis (Candy Stick Tellin)
1"

Tellina carpenteri (Carpenter's Tellin)
<1"

Macoma balthica (Balthic macoma)
½~1½"

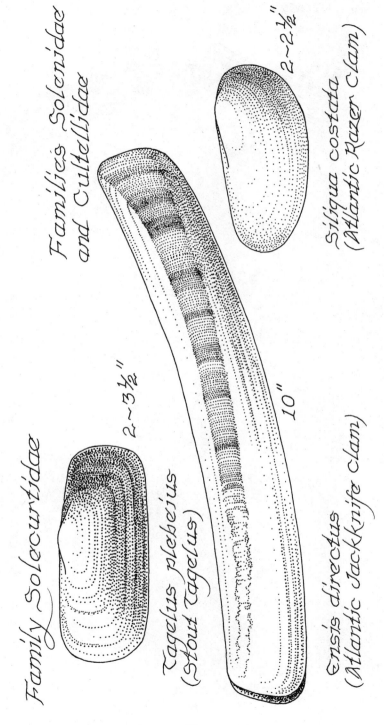

Family Solecurtidae

Families Solenidae
and Cultellidae

2~3½"

Tagelus plebeius
(Stout Tagelus)

10"

Ensis directus
(Atlantic Jackknife Clam)

2~2½"

Siliqua costata
(Atlantic Razor Clam)

33

Family Mactridae

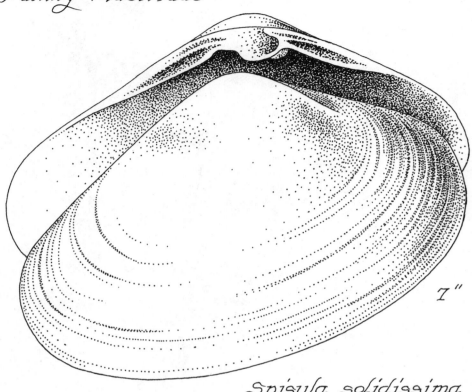

7"

Spisula solidissima
(Atlantic Surf Clam)

Family Myidae

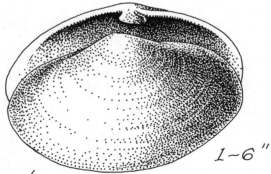

1~6"

Mya arenaria
(Common Soft-shelled
or Steamer Clam)

Crytopleura costata
(Angel Wings)

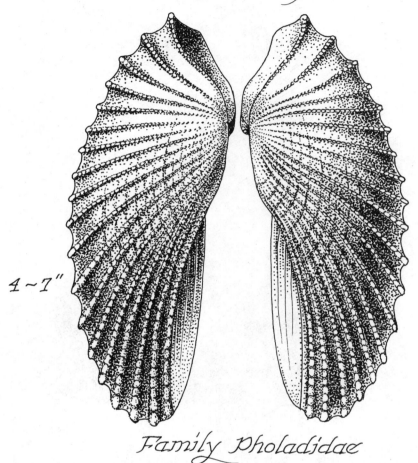

4 ~ 7"

Family Pholadidae

The **Pink Conch** (also known as the Queen Conch), about 8 to 12 inches, is a shell found in South Florida and the West Indies. You'll see empty Conch Shells piled up all over shores in the Bahamas. Conch is a national dish in the Bahamas.

The **Florida Fighting Conch**, 2 to 3 inches, can be found in southwest Pacific waters.

SLIPPER SHELLS

The **Common Atlantic Slipper** shell, about ¾ to 2 inches is so common it can be found all over in warmer, temperate seas.

PERIWINKLES

Periwinkles, from ½ to 1 inch, can be found on rocky shores nearly everywhere.

Superfamily Fissurellacea

Family Acmaeidae

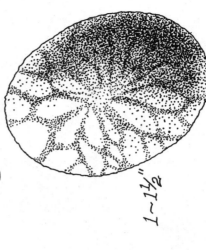

1~1½"

Collisella testudinalis
(Atlantic plate Limpet)

2½~5"

Fissurella crenulata
(Giant Keyhole Limpet)

1"

Fissurella barbadensis
(Barbados Keyhole Limpet)

36

Family Trochidae

Clanculus sp.
(Strawberry Top)

1"

Cittarium pica
(West Indian Top)

3"

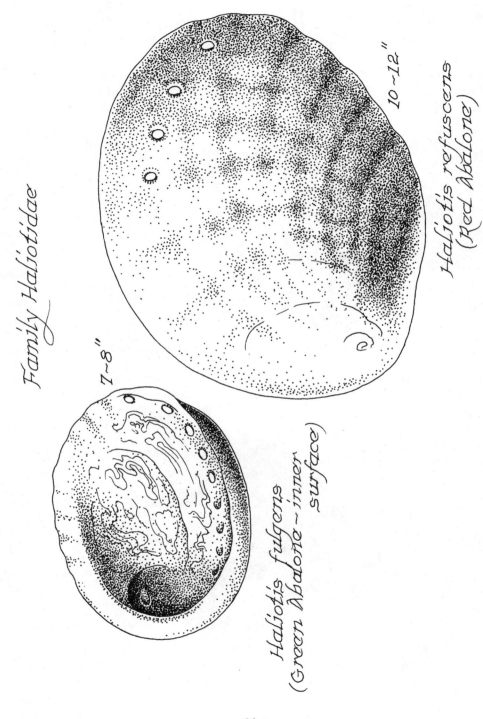

Family Haliotidae

Haliotis refuscens
(Red Abalone)

10~12"

7~8"

Haliotis fulgens
(Green Abalone~inner
surface)

38

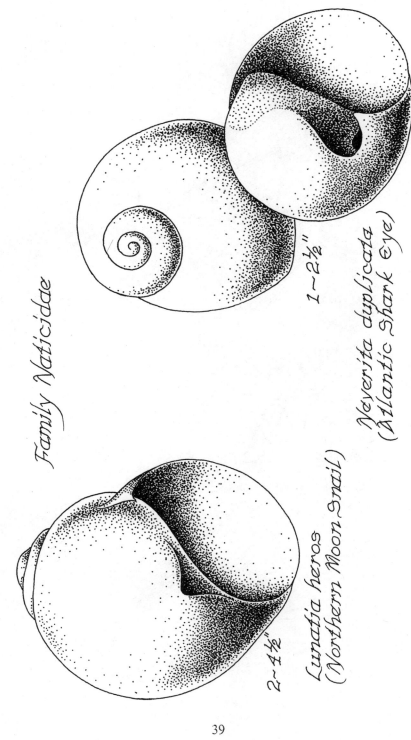

Family Naticidae

Neverita duplicata
(Atlantic Shark Eye)

1~2½"

Lunatia heros
(Northern Moon Snail)

2~4½"

39

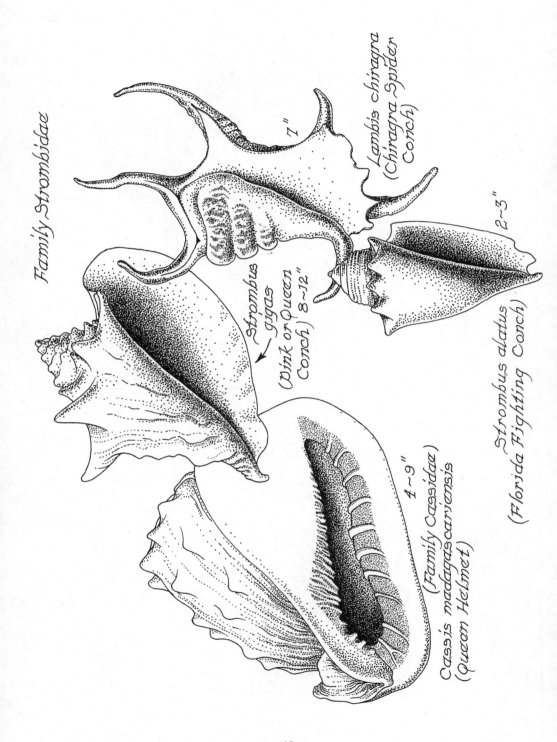

Family Strombidae

Lambis chiragra
(Chiragra Spider
Conch)

7"

Strombus gigas
(Pink or Queen
Conch) 8-12"

Strombus alatus
(Florida Fighting Conch)

2-3"

4-9"
(Family Cassidae)
Cassis madagascariensis
(Queen Helmet)

Family Littorinidae

 ½" *Nodilittorina tuberculata*
Common Prickly-winkle)

 ½" *Littorina ziczac*
(Ziczac periwinkle)

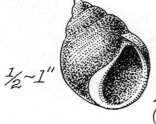 ½~1" *Littorina littorea*
(Common periwinkle)

Family Crepidulidae

 ¾~2"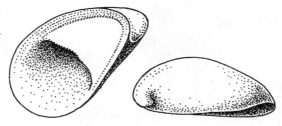

Crepidula fornicata
(Common Slipper Shell)

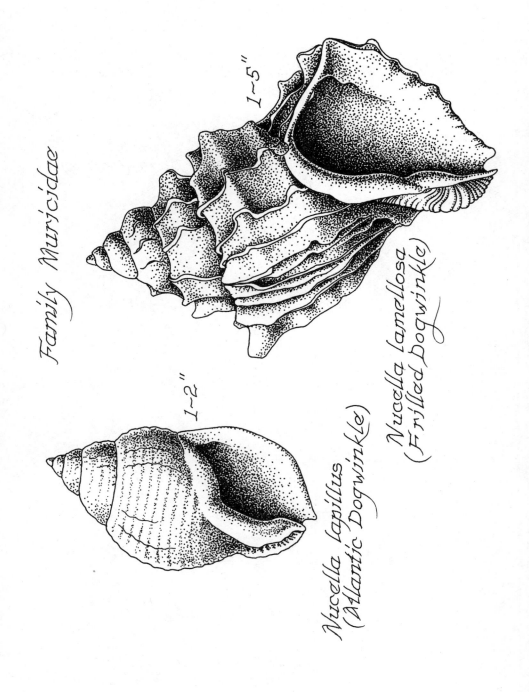

Family Muricidae

1~5"

Nucella lamellosa
(Frilled Dogwinkle)

1~2"

Nucella lapillus
(Atlantic Dogwinkle)

Family Melongenidae

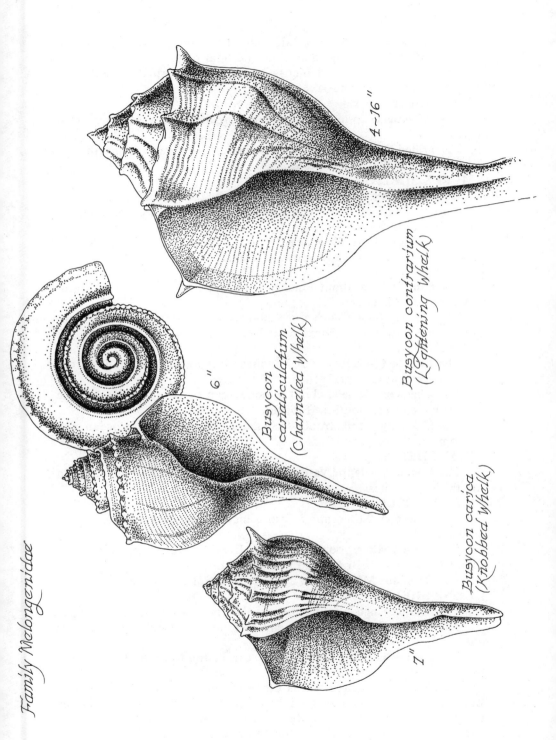

Busycon canaliculatum
(Channeled Whelk)
6"

Busycon contrarium
(Lightening Whelk)
4~16"

Busycon carica
(Knobbed Whelk)
7"

43

The **Ziczac periwinkle**, .7 of an inch, of Southeast Florida, the West Indies, and Bermuda is abundant on intertidal rocks.

The slightly smaller (.5 inch) **Common Prickly-winkle** is native to South Florida and Bermuda.

DOGWINKLES

The **Atlantic Dogwinkle**, about 1 to 2 inches, is an Atlantic Coast shell.

The **Frilled Dogwinkle**, about 1 to 5 inches, is native to the northwestern coastline of the United States.

MUREX SHELLS

Carbit's Murex, about 2 to 3 inches, can be found in Florida and the West Indies. There are, however, many other varieties of murex shells.

DOVE SHELLS

The **Common Dove Shell**, about ½ to ¾ inch, lives in Florida, Bermuda, and the West Indies and south to Brazil.

TULIP SHELLS

The **Banded Tulip**, about 3 inches, lives in the Atlantic from the Carolinas south to Texas.

The **Florida Horse Conch**, up to 20 inches, can be found in the Atlantic from the Carolinas to Mexico offshore.

WHELKS

The **Knobbed Whelk**, about 7 inches, lives along the Atlantic from Massachusetts to Georgia.

The **Channeled Whelk**, about 6 inches, can be found in the Atlantic from Massachusetts south to Florida.

The **Lightning Whelk**, from 4 to 16 inches, can be found in ocean waters from the Carolinas to Texas.

VASE SHELLS

The **Common Atlantic Vase**, about 4 inches, can be found in Florida and the West Indies.

MITER SHELLS

The **Episcopal Miter**, about 3 to 5 inches, can be found on Pacific coral reefs.

The **Beaded Miter**, about ¾ to 1 inch, lives on shores from North Carolina to Florida and Brazil and in Bermuda.

The **Barbados Miter**, about 2 inches, is a Caribbean shell.

CONE SHELLS

The **Marble Cone**, about 4 inches, also lives on Pacific coral reefs.

The **Florida Cone**, 1½ inches, can be found in Florida and the West Indies.

The **California Cone**, 1 to 2 inches, can be found in the Pacific from Panama north to California.

Special Note: Bob Sicada warns other readers in a letter to *Yachting World* (December 1987) that all **Red Sea cone shells** produce venom. Some can be fatal to humans. He suggests that divers new to the area get information about local marine life before collecting shells there.

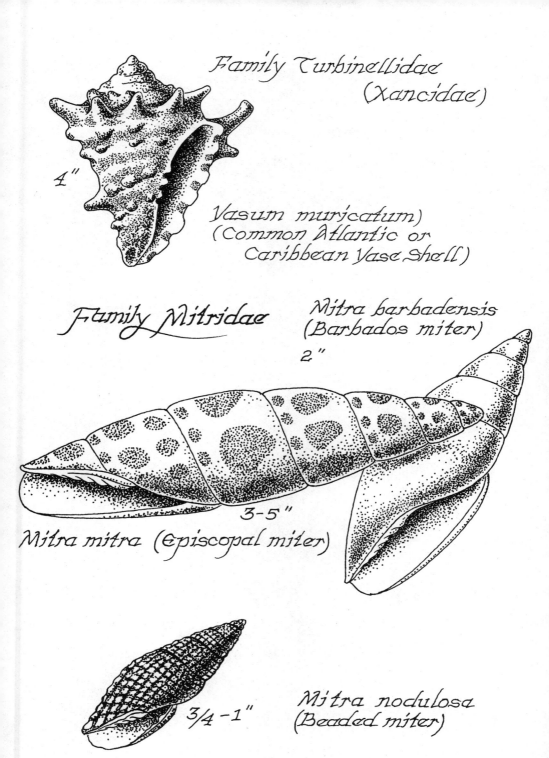

Family Turbinellidae
(Xancidae)

4"

Vasum muricatum)
(Common Atlantic or
Caribbean Vase Shell)

Family Mitridae

Mitra barbadensis
(Barbados miter)
2"

3-5"

Mitra mitra (Episcopal miter)

3/4 - 1"

Mitra nodulosa
(Beaded miter)

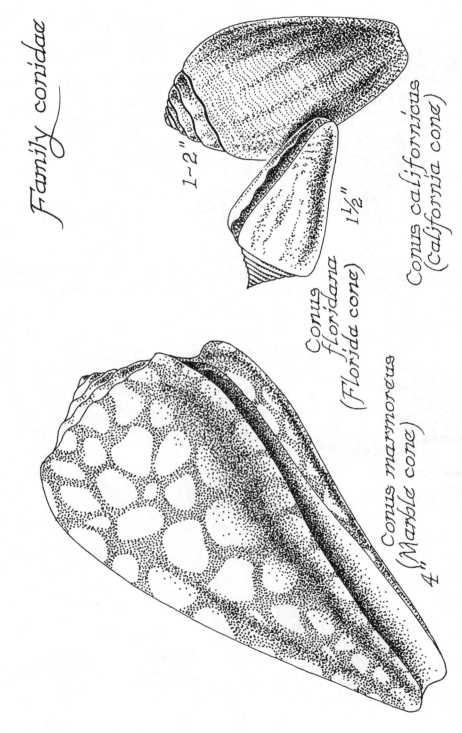

Family conidae

1-2"

Conus floridana
(Florida cone)   1½"

Conus californicus
(California cone)

Conus marmoreus
(Marble cone)
4"

Family Argonautidae

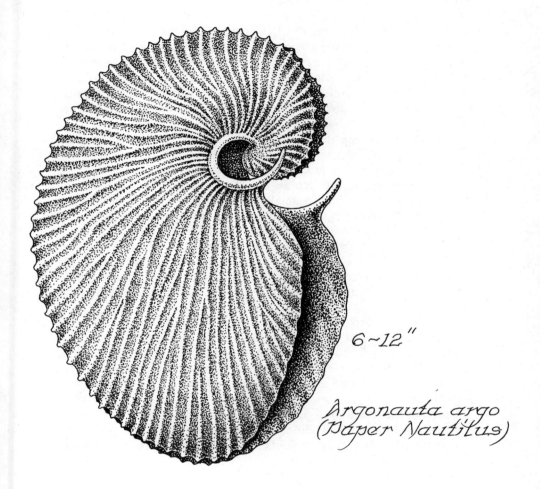

6~12"

Argonauta argo
(Paper Nautilus)

TOOTH SHELLS (Scaphopoda)
    The **Money Tusk**, about 1 to 2 inches, can be found along Pacific coasts from Alaska south to California.
    PAPER NAUTILUS (Cephalopoda)
    The **Paper Nautilus**, from 6 to 12 inches, lives worldwide in warm seas.

SEA PLANTS AND ANIMALS

Starfish, Sand Dollars, and Sea Urchins

Starfish, sand dollars, and **sea urchins,** actually are relatives of the **sea cucumber,** are all echinoderms. **Echinoderms** are easily recognizable many times because most have spines for defending themselves on the outside of their bodies. These spines, however, may be missing from these animals when you find their empty, bleached shells on the beach.

Six thousand species of echinoderms live in seas all over the world from the intertidal zone to the ocean depths in all latitudes from the tropics to the poles.

Two thousand of these are varieties of starfish, some of which are common along the shores of the Atlantic and the Pacific in temperate zones. In other areas, starfish are more apt to be picked up in fishnets. Starfish can vary in size, color, and details. For example, some starfish in deep water can grow up to 3 feet. A smaller starfish (about 10 inches across) which can be found in the Great Barrier Reef of Australia is bright blue.

The 750 species of sea urchins and sand dollars vary as well. One sea urchin common in North Atlantic has dark green or blue-green spines while those of another variety in the warm waters of the South Pacific are black and white, making this sea urchin look like a tiny sea procupine. Deep water sea urchins may grow up to 98 feet. Their spines may be ½ thick or more.

The starfish, sea urchins, and sand dollars shown here may not be exactly like the ones you will find in your area, but they will generally ressemble each other. You can expect, however, that starfish found in tide pools and shallow water will be considerably smaller than those picked up by fishermen or scuba divers in deeper waters.

STARFISH
   Common Eastern Star, 6–11″, Maine to Gulf of Mexico
   Sunflower Star to 30″, Pacific: Alaska to San Diego
   Common Sun Star to 14″, Atlantic: Arctic south to New Jersey. Pacific: Arctic south to Vancouver.
SEA URCHINS
   Sea urchin with spines still attached, and sea urchin shell after spines have fallen off.
SAND DOLLARS
   Atlantic Sand Dollar 2–3″
   Notched Sand Dollar 2–3″

Lobsters and Crabs

Lobsters and crabs, both members of the **phylum Crustacea,** are scavengers. They come in many varieties and can be found throughout the world.

True lobsters inhabit cooler waters and have great commercial value. Especially favored is the Maine lobster, which can also be found in the

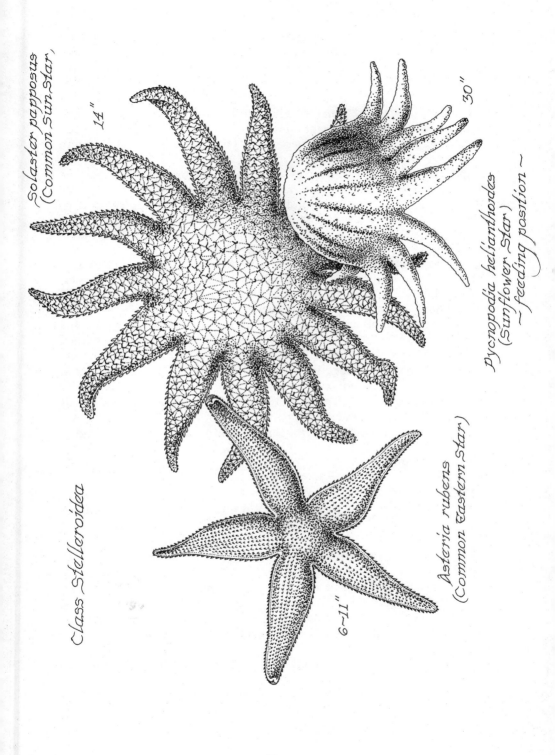

Class Stellaroidea

Solaster papposus
(Common Sun Star)

14"

Pycnopodia helianthoides
(Sunflower Star)
~ feeding position ~

30"

Asteria rubens
(Common Eastern Star)

6~11"

49

cool waters of other New England states and Canada. These lobsters are flown live everywhere, and now appear on the menus in gourmet restaurants all over the world. They have large front claws and can grow up to 2 feet. perhaps the heaviest lobster ever found of this type weighed in at 41½ pounds!

American lobsters are generally found from Southern Labrador to Cape Hatteras. The **European lobster** lives from Norway to the Mediterranean Sea. **Norway, or Dublin Bay, lobsters** inhabit the cooler waters of Northern Europe.

Spiny lobsters (also known as crayfish or langouste), who have no claws, prefer coral reefs, rocks, and sandy bottoms of sheltered areas. There are about 45 species found primarily in tropical and subtropical latitudes although a few do live in some temperate regions.

A third type of lobster known as the **slipper or mud lobster** lives buried in mud or sand in shallow, warm waters worldwide.

Deepsea lobsters are generally less well-known than the others because they live at great depths buried in muddy bottoms. These deapsea lobsters are blind and, surprisingly, fossils of these animals were found long before anyone discovered any living specimens!

There are 47 families of crabs. They live mainly on sea bottoms and walk on the sea bed. A few are swimmers. FLorida's **stone crabs** with their large, hard front claws are really **hermit crabs**, relative to the tiny hermit crabs found at water's edge living in shells formerly inhabited by snails and other marine animals.

Rock Crab lives from New England to South Carolina. Another variety lives in waters on the Pacific Coast.

Green (or Blue) Crab lives all over the world on rocky shores and in estuaries from Brazil to North America, in Europe, North Africa, Sri Lanka, Australia, and Hawaii. It is most active at night and at high tide, moving upshore with the tide.

Male Fiddler Crab with enlarged claw. This crab lives on the coast and in salt marshes from New England to Florida. Similar varieties can be found on the Pacific shores.

Other Sea Animals and Plants

Here are some examples of other sea plants and animals you'll find in some form nearly everywhere. (Drawings for these)

The **HORSE SHOE CRAB** from the coast of North America is pictured here. Sometimes you'll find only the empty shell of the horse shoe crab. Other times all its innards will still be attached. Another variety found in Southeast Asia can grow up to 2 feet long. Horse shoe crabs are not true crabs. They are more closely related to **spiders** than to the crabs described earlier.

SPONGES are the most primitive of multicellular animals. They have porous bodies and live in all seas. There are many varieties of sponges. The one shown here is called **Deadman's Fingers**.

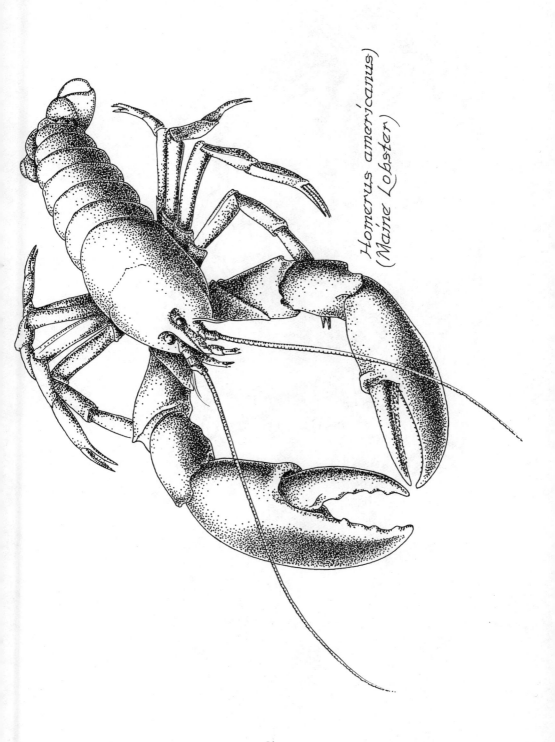

Homerus americanus
(Maine Lobster)

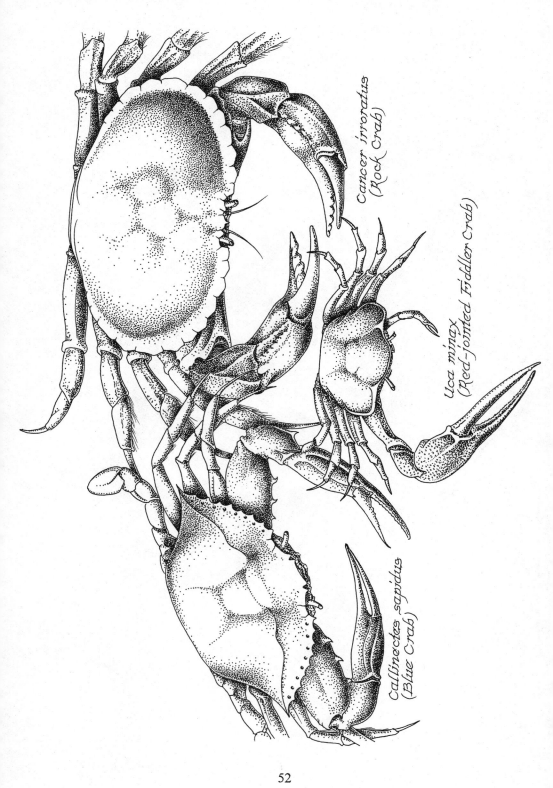

Cancer irroratus
(Rock Crab)

Uca minax
(Red-jointed Fiddler Crab)

Callinectes sapidus
(Blue Crab)

52

CORAL   Two examples of coral. There are many varieties! Coral is found in warm waters all over the world. In the Atlantic coral lives north as far as Bermuda.

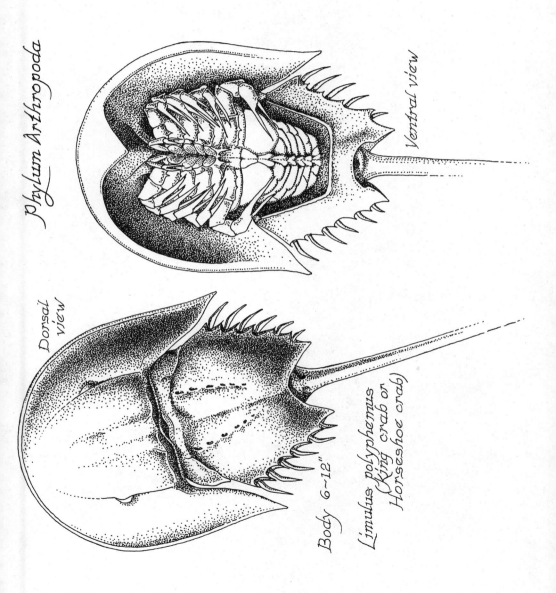

Phylum Arthropoda

Ventral view

Dorsal view

Body 6-12"

Limulus polyphemus
(King crab or
Horseshoe crab)

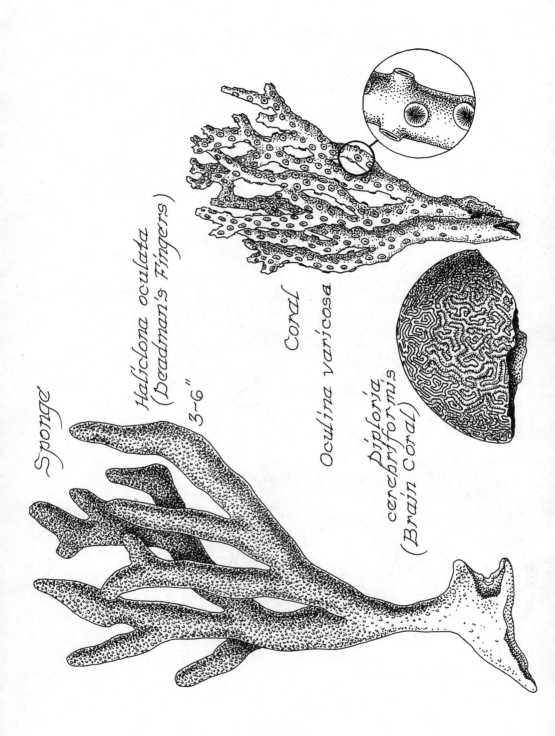

Sponge

Haliclona oculata
(Deadman's Fingers)
3–6"

Coral

Oculina varicosa

*Diploria
cerebriformis*
(Brain Coral)

PART II: BEACHCRAFTING

INTRODUCTION

Now that you have collected all kinds of shells, glass, and other treasures from your beachcombing trips, you'll want to do more with them than just fill up storage space. Beachcrafting will not only give you an interesting way to spend a rainy summer afternoon or the long, cold winter evenings but will also provide you with some unique handmade gifts for family and friends. Once you begin making some of the items described in this book, your own creativity may lead you to some clever inventions of your own. You may even want to make a few extra dollars by selling your handicrafts.

Perhaps you'd like to display your hobby at shows or fairs. In addition to craft shows nearly everywhere, there are shows where shell collectors and shell crafters can compete for prizes. These occur most commonly in the fall, before the holiday season. One of the oldest has been held each February in Sanibel, Florida, since 1937. The Sanibel Shell Fair is divided into two divisions: Scientific (for collectors) and Artistic (for craftspeople). There are separate categories in each division so that beginners don't have to compete against others with a great deal of experience. If you'd like to use your hobby as an excuse for a winter trip to Florida next year, write to the Sanibel Community Association, P.O. Box 76, Sanibel, Florida 33957, for further details about the annual fair.

CHAPTER 4

CLEANING THE BEACHCOMBING BOOTY TO USE IN CRAFTS

BEACH GLASS

Beach glass can be washed or scrubbed with any detergent. A little elbow grease and a mildly abrasive cleaner will remove most dirt and stains. Beach glass is more apt to be damaged by dumping it from one place to another than by cleaning.

If you wish, you can wipe glass in a finished craft with mineral oil to give a "wet" look, but don't put the oil on until **after** you have glued it or the glue might not stick.

SHELLS

If you have collected shells which are not empty, dry them outside for several days until the insides of the shells can be washed clean. You won't want to dry shells in the house because some have a very unpleasant order while they are drying out. While on sailboat cruising trips your editor lets smelly shells dry off on the transom, but too often, offended crew members give them the deep-six! If you have an ant hill in your yard, you can leave the shells on top of it and the ants will help by eating what's left of the animals inside. Burying in soft sand for two weeks will allow the animals to rot. When the shells have been thoroughly dried, rotted, or picked clean by ants, check the insides. Clean out any remaining debris, using a needle or nut/lobster pick if needed, and then wash them in warm water and detergent.

If you don't have time to deal with shells of living animals when you bring them home, you can store them in the refrigerator for a day before cleaning them. Although tropical animals will die quickly, cold water specimens may live for several days in your refrigerator.

Shells can also be soaked for a few days in either ethyl or isopropyl alcohol, or boiled in water—if you're in a hurry to use the shells. Stains on the outside can be scrubbed with a mildly abrasive cleaner or soaked in a solution of bleach and water. Be careful with the bleach though. I soaked some beautifully colored shells in a weak solution of bleach and water to get rid of an unpleasant odor only to discover later that the bleach caused the bright colors to fade. Soaking shells in baking soda and water will eliminate a smell without any damage to shells.

Your freezer offers another possibility for cleaning shells. Put the living specimens in a plastic bowl with a paper towel folded inside on the bottom to collect any water which drains from them. Leave them in the freezer for at least three days. When you take them out, run cool (not hot) water over them. Then pick the insides out with a needle or nut pick and wash them gently in a mild detergent and water.

Other solutions, such as formalin, lye, and muriatic acid may be used to clean shells, but they require special precautions. Acid and lye, for example, will destroy the operculum along with the animal tissue inside and can burn your skin as well, if you're not careful. The shell-cleaning methods described above are safer both for you and the shells than formalin, lye, or muriatic acid.

If you intend to use your shells to build a shell collection rather than to use them in crafts, you must be very careful not to damage the shells as you clean them. Avoid such harsh methods as boiling them. Save the operculum, the "little door" on snail shells, for example. Remove the operculum carefully and when your shell is clean and dry, stuff the empty shell with cotton and glue the operculum back in place.

To put a sheen on your shells, rub with mineral oil, but remember not to put oil on if your shells will be used in a craft project. The oil may prevent the glue from bonding. When the craft is finished, you can then oil the shells, if desired.

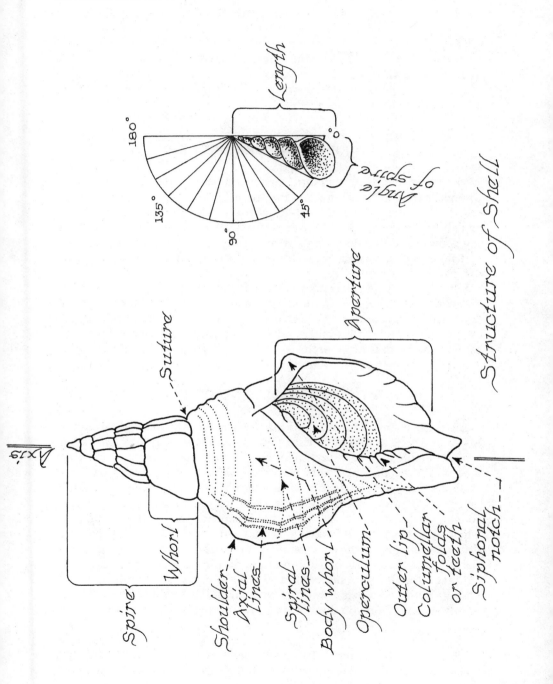

Structure of Shell

Length

Angle of spire

0°

45°

90°

135°

180°

Suture

Aperture

Axis

Spire

Whorl

Shoulder

Axial Lines

Spiral Lines

Body whorl

Operculum

Outer lip

Columellar folds or teeth

Siphonal notch

CRABS

Small, dead crabs which you find washed up on the shore or those that you have dried outside for a few days need to be handled carefully or they will fall apart. If a claw has fallen off, glue it back to the body. Then with a small brush, carefully cover the whole crab with a coat of clear varnish. After the varnish is dry, the crab may be used in a table or other craft. If your crab is in good condition, you can dip it in polyurethane instead of varnishing it with a brush.

STARFISH AND SEA URCHINS

Starfish dried outside may turn mushy and become flat and unattractive. To make sure your starfish don't lose their looks, bake them on a cookie sheet in a 400 degree oven for 5–10 minutes. Watch them to be sure they don't burn and be prepared for an unusual odor while they are baking. If you want the starfish to dry in a special shape, you must arrange them in that shape before baking or air drying. See the directions for making starfish people in Chapter 10.

John Ross, whose creations you'll see in Chapter 10, soaks almost all of his shells, including sea urchins, in bleach and water. He then lets them dry outside for several days before using them in crafts. He cautions, however, that sea urchins lose their spines when soaked in bleach and water so if you want to use the urchins with spines, let them dry naturally.

FISHNET, DRIFTWOOD, AND OTHER ITEMS

Anything else you have found may be rinsed with fresh water and allowed to dry naturally outside. If your fishnet is too dirty or smells bad, soak it outside for a few days in a pan of detergent, perhaps with a small amount of bleach. Then rinse with clear water and dry on a line.

Be careful washing driftwood and don't use any bleach on a fragile piece of driftwood. Some wood has been soaked by salt water and dried so many times at the water's edge that it is rotten inside. It may fall apart when you clean it. Realize, too, that the beautiful silvery color of driftwood is only on the surface of the wood and you can very easily lose that natural finish just be rubbing or scrubbing the wood too briskly.

Make sure all of the materials you plan to use in your crafts are clean and dry before you begin working with them. Glue won't adhere to a wet or oily surface. And you don't want your finished project to give off a foul odor.

If you get involved in making crafts on a regular basis, you can store shells, beach glass, and driftwood outside where the weather will help clean them for you. You may also wish to "weather" your own boards to use as backings for wall hangings or as bases for driftwood lamps. If you don't live in a warm climate, however, and you plan to use any of these items for crafts during the middle of winter, make sure they're accessible when snow covers the ground!

Round cocktail table with glass removed for photo

CHAPTER FIVE

TURNING THE TIDE INTO TABLES

Would you like an unusual table for your deck, porch, family room, or dining room? Beachcombing provides all kinds of materials for making tables. Cocktail tables can be made from driftwood or lobster traps, or you can display all of your beachcombing treasures in a table that you design yourself for your dining area or living room.

LOBSTER TRAP TABLES

Lobster trap tables are easy to make. Find a weathered trap in good condition with a flat top. Traps also come with round tops which can be used for tables if you turn them up on end. You can use the trap as it is for a cocktail table indoors or out. However, in order to have a smooth surface, one that's safer for holding glasses and cups, you may wish to add a glass top. Measure the top of the trap and have a piece of glass or plexiglass cut to fit. You don't need to attach the glass permanently to the trap. The weight of the glass itself will do a good job of holding the top in place. However, plexiglass tops should be glued to the trap with epoxy. If you get your trap directly from a lobsterman, it may come with barnacle-encrusted rocks (which were used as weights) inside and some captive shells, authentic reminders of the lobster trap's working past.

DRIFTWOOD TABLES

Driftwood tables can be made much the same way. Find a sturdy, interesting piece of driftwood which is suitably shaped for holding a glass top. You may have to put more than one piece of driftwood together to create the base. To give the table more stability, use a flat board on the bottom, stained or antiqued to blend in with the color of your driftwood. Nail the driftwood to the base and set the glass on the top of the driftwood. For added security you may also wish to use epoxy to glue the glass in place where it touches the driftwood.

GLASS TOP BEACHCOMBER'S DISPLAY TABLES

Glass top beachcomber's display tables are just what the name implies: a show case for your best beachcombing finds. You may purchase a table, have one made, or make it yourself. Then choose your best treasures from the shore to display under the glass top.

Lobster Trap and Driftwood Tables

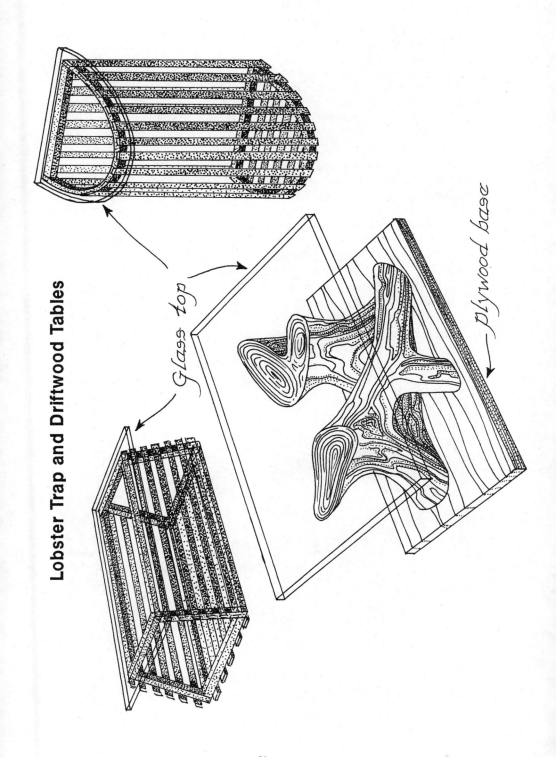

Glass top

Plywood base

The tables you can buy ready-to-use are usually designed as end or side tables, often of dark wood, finished to match standard living room furniture. Look in your local furniture store or in mail order catalogs if you want a table which is ready to fill. And keep your eyes open! My neighbor got a good buy on a small curio table for her living room when the hospital gift shop where she did volunteer work no longer needed it for display.

If you want a more informal-looking table which you can stain or antique to look like driftwood, you may be able to purchase one from a store which specializes in ready-to-finish furniture. If you can't find one ready-made in the size and style you desire, you'll have to plan your own table.

You can get complete plans for making a cocktail table with a hinged glass top published by the Stanley Work Company at your hardware store or by mail: Advertising Services, The Stanley Works, Box 1800, New Britain, CT 06050. Ask for brochures entitled "The Stanley Collector's Table" or "Stanley Collectible Display Ideas." The second brochure also includes other storage and display ideas in addition to plans for the table.

If you want to design your own table and have it made to order as I did, first decide what size and shape you want. Tables to be used as dining, cocktail, or end tables, can be round, square, or rectangular. My first table, which I used in the kitchen for dining, was round, 28″ high and 48″ in diameter. When I later decided that a rectangular one would be more practical, I had one made, which measures 40″ by 60″. In my living room I have a cocktail table, which is round, but only 15½″ high and 30″ in diameter. The basic table design is kind of a wooden tray, from 3–6″ deep, with legs.

Rectangular cocktail tables (glass removed for photo)
displays stones and shards collected by author on foreign travels

Edge of dining table shows wood lip extending out to support rope

On all three tables I wound heavy rope around the outer edge of the "tray" top. Inside, the bottom of the "tray" is covered with a layer of sand on which shells, beach glass, rocks, bits of fishnet, cork floats, starfish, tiny crabs, and sand dollars are strewn so they appear to have been washed up on the sand.

If you are handy with wood, you could make the table base yourself. Otherwise, a carpenter or cabinetmaker can craft a base to your specifications.

If you plan to use rope as trim around the outside of the top, have the table base made so that a lip extends out from the bottom on which the rope can rest. We didn't do that on the first table, and the rope kept coming loose. You can purchase heavy rope at a marine supply store. On the dining table I used ¾ inch rope, but half-inch rope looked better on the smaller cocktail table. Decide first what diameter the rope will be so that the lip on the table can be made to match the diameter of the rope you choose. Use tiny nails and glue to hold the rope to the side of the table top. The lip will keep the bottom layer of rope from falling down. Even though you must plan for the rope before you build your table, don't attach the rope to the table until the wood has been finished and is completely dry.

The glass for the top of the table should be cut to cover the edges of the table and extend over the rope as well. Therefore, have the glass cut slightly larger than the area of the top of your wooden base. It should match the area of the bottom which includes the extended lip for the rope. If you're making a large round table and need something in the center of the table to help support the weight of the glass top, you can use cork floats. If two floats stacked one on top of the other are too high, slice one of the floats to get the thickness you need.

I have left the glass loose on the top of the tables so that I can lift it to add more items to the tables and to occasionally clean the underside. It's heavy enough to stay put. When I later had a rectangular cocktail table built to display the rocks I had collected from my travels, I changed the top design slightly so that the glass is inset on the beveled edges of the wood sides, but it is still not permanently attached. To remove the glass top from this table, I use a suction cup to lift one corner high enough to get my hand under it.

If you want the finish on the table to look like driftwood, you may want to experiment to get just the effect you want. I antiqued the first two tables, using a white base coat with gray stain. When I was ready to finish the last one, however, I decided to use only a blue-gray stain which the man in the paint store custom-mixed for me. We spent about an hour mixing and testing colors to get just the shade I wanted.

Customize chairs to match your table

A dining table needs chairs. From a store which sells unfinished furniture, you can buy straight-backed, captain's, mate's, or director's chairs which can be stained or antiqued to match the wood on your table. Be-

This shows how table edge can be beveled so that glass top is inset

64

**Dining room table. The hanging lamp above
is decorated with colorful beach glass**

cause director's chairs are often used on boats and decks of summer
houses, they are in keeping with the sea image of the table and you have
the additional advantage of being able to buy canvas material in a variety
of colors and design to make chair seats and backs to blend with your decor.

Construction of Placemats

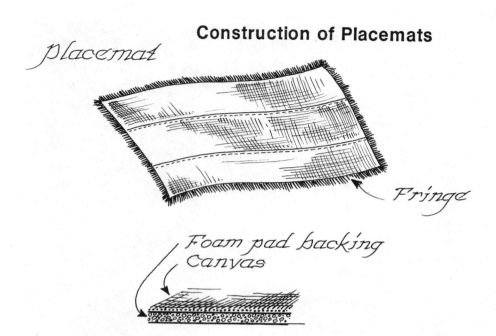

Placemat

Fringe

Foam pad backing
Canvas

Add matching placemats

If you do choose director's chairs and decide to make new seats and backs, get some extra yardage when you buy the canvas and make matching placemats. You will also need some foam-backed table padding, the kind you buy in a package and cut to fit your table.

Make a pattern for your placemat from newspaper. You can trace around a placemat you already have, or cut the newspaper and try it out on your table. For each placemat, cut two pieces of canvas (or one piece if you don't want reversible mats) and one piece of table padding. Trim the table padding to be about ½ to one inch smaller all around than the canvas pieces, so it won't show on the edges of the finished placemat. Then sandwich the table padding between the two pieces of canvas and machine stitch around the placemat about ½ inch from the edges. Finish the edges of the placemats by raveling the material evenly into a fringe on all sides.

TWO OTHER TABLE DESIGNS

Here are two more possibilities for refurbishing an old table or making a new one.

If you like working with polyester casting resin, measure your table to see how may tiles of what size you will need to cover it. Then get molds from a craft store or use flexible plastic food containers to make tiles the size you want. Arrange shells, sea glass, or other treasures on a sheet of newspaper cut to match the size and shape of your table. Then, following the directions which come with the resin, fill the molds, add the catalyst, and stir. Move your sells or sea glass from the newspaper pattern to the corresponding locations in the mold. Let dry. When the tiles are ready, glue them to the top of your table with epoxy.

If you have an old table of soft wood, you can dress it up by gouging out areas of the top for shells or pieces of beach glass. Your holes should be deep enough so that shells or glass are level with the rest of the table top. Glue these items directly to the wood. Then cover with several coasts of polyurethane, making sure that each coat is completely dry before you put on the next. Your table top will be indestructible and unique.

Add any one of these tables to your home, and you can enjoy the beach all twelve months of the year!

Candle holders have been screwed into this piece of driftwood

CHAPTER 6

CANDLE CRAFTS

You can have fun using shells, beach glass, cork floats, and driftwood to make several types of attractive candleholders. A quahog shell is the perfect size to hold a votive candle and, if it's clean, it's all ready to use as is. When they need inexpensive chandleholders for several tables at a potluck supper, most people use Chianti wine bottles or dime store variety glass stars. Instead, you can easily and quickly make cork float candleholders to grace the tables during the meal and give as favors to guests when they leave. Beach glass candleholders are special enough for gifts, while driftwood can serve as a centerpiece as well as a holder for candles.

USING CORK FLOATS, CORAL, OR DRIFTWOOD

Except for decoration, a cork float is ready to use. Just insert a candle in the hole in the center. Glue shells or small pieces of beach glass on the float for an extra touch.

Some pieces of coral may be just the right size and shape to hold candles. However, you might want to mount the coral on a piece of driftwood to keep melting wax from dripping through spaces in the coral onto your furniture.

If you want to use driftwood, find a piece sturdy enough and shaped so that it will hold a candle. Hollow out a hole in the driftwood just large and deep enough to hold the candle. Then glue small shells, starfish, sand dollars, or pieces of beach glass to the driftwood. Put the candle in its hole, and you've got an inexpensive candleholder to remind you of the ocean. Instead of making holes in the driftwood, you can purchase metal or wooden candleholders. These can be screwed in or glued to the driftwood. Check your local crafts shop for these.

These candleholders can be made in pairs, or several candles can be mounted in a larger piece of driftwood, making a unique centerpiece for your dinner table. If the shape of your driftwood permits, you can set a vase of freshly cut flowers in the middle of the wood between two candles.

AN EASY DESIGN USING BEACH GLASS

Beach glass, clear glue, and a little ingenuity are all it takes to easily make this striking beach glass candleholder. You need a large piece of beach glass about 3"–4" in diameter to use for a base and several smaller pieces to glue on it around the candle. A wide candle, 2" or more in diameter, looks best.

A beach glass base covered with smaller
pieces of beach glass holds a large candle

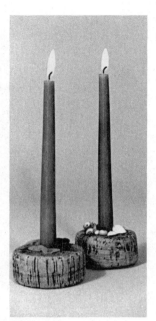

Cork float candle holders. One is decorated
with beach glass, the other with shells

First find a candle of the appropriate size for your base and place it in the middle of the large piece of beach glass. Make sure it will stand up straight by itself. If it doesn't, glue small pieces of beach glass under the candle to make it level. Draw a faint line on the glass, around the candle, with a felt tip pen or pencil. Then put the candle aside.

Using craft glue which will dry clear, glue small pieces of different colored beach glass to the base, covering the whole area **except** the spot which has been reserved for the candle. You can vary this design slightly by using sand to outline the piece of beach glass, giving the impression they have been embedded in the sand. To do this, put glue between each piece of glass as well as under it. Do not put glue in the center area reserved for the candle. While the glue is still wet, strain sand over the whole candleholder. When the glue is dry, shake off all the loose sand.

When the base is finished, melt the wax on the bottom of the candle slightly before you place it in the center of the base. The wax will harden again, making the candle a little more secure on its base. Your unique beach glass candleholder is ready to light.

USING BEACH GLASS TO RESEMBLE STAINED GLASS

Candleholders or vases covered with beach glass to give the effect of stained glass are stunning and unusual. The epoxy that you use to attach

69

Candles burning inside a jar that has been covered with
beach glass attached with epoxy to give a stained glass effect

the beach glass to the base outlines each piece of glass. This is the same
way that lead makes outlines in the stained glass art work found in the
world's most beautiful cathedrals, such as Notre Dame de Chartres or
Paris. The designs you create will be original. Materials needed to make
this candleholder include a clear jar or vase for the base, beach glass, and
epoxy.

First find a jar or vase of fairly heavy, clear glass in the size and shape
you prefer for the base. The finished candleholder will be the same shape
as the base you choose. Look in your grocery store for the preserves which
come in a small square jar with a round top: a jar of this shape makes a
very beautiful beach glass candleholder. I have used fairly heavy drink-
ing glasses, peanut butter jars, and the like as bases. Be sure to use clear
glass rather than colored so the colors of the beach glass remain true
when the candle is lighted.

Next purchase epoxy from the hardware or building supplies store. The
right epoxy is very important, since it will look on the finished
candleholder the same way that lead does in a stained glass window. Get
the type used for mending pipes. PC-7 (manufactured by Protective Coating Co., Allentown, PA 18103) in paste form is one brand name for which
you can ask. The epoxy comes in two parts and must be mixed together
before you can use it. The material in one can is black; in the other, gray.
Although the directions say to mix equal parts of each color, you will
have a more attractive candleholder if you use a little more black than
gray.

Before you begin working, in addition to the epoxy, gather your beach
glass, some cotton swabs, acetone or an epoxy thinner, an old knife, plenty of sturdy toothpicks—cocktail toothpicks will work best—and a couple
of rags. Get a piece of cardboard on which to mix the epoxy so you won't

70

have to worry about cleaning up. Spread newspapers on your working surface and place your base and a large pile of beach glass where you can reach it easily. You should have more pieces of beach glass than you will actually use so that you can find just the right shapes, sizes, or colors you will need as you create your own design.

Take small amounts of both black and gray epoxy and put them together on the board. Use the knife to mix them together until the mixture is uniform in color. Mix only a small amount of epoxy at a time so that you will use all that you've mixed before it dries and you won't have any left over when you quit working for the day. You can work with the epoxy you've mixed for a half-hour, maybe longer on cool days, but to avoid having too much mixed, I usually work with small batches.

Choose a piece of beach glass and hold it against the candleholder base. Use a toothpick to pick up a small amount of epoxy and smooth it around the outside edges of the piece of glass so that it sticks to the surface of the base. Because the epoxy, although sticky, has a consistency like clay, you can use the toothpick to shape the expoy as you work with it. Be careful not to stick your fingers in the epoxy as you work. Continue the same process as you add each additional piece of glass to your base.

As you select pieces of glass, remember to vary the colors and shapes. Your candleholder could be a random arrangement of multi-colored beach glass, or you can select colors so that you create a design. Use extra epoxy to fill in between the pieces of glass, covering uneven or awkward edges when necessary. Beach glass with sharp edges can be used for this candleholder since the epoxy covers the entire outside edge of each piece of glass. If you accidentally get epoxy on the center of a piece of glass or if you wish to push the epoxy back further to expose more of the glass, wet a cotton swab in the acetone or thinner and wipe off the excess epoxy. As long as it has not dried, the same solution will remove epoxy from your hands or tools as well.

As you are attaching glass to the base, be careful that a piece does not come loose before it dries. Work only on **one** side at a time and let the area dry completely before you turn the candleholder. Why is this precaution necessary? Some pieces of glass may be too heavy to be held in place by the wet epoxy, and may move or fall off when you begin working on the other side. Finding a place for your fingers to hold the candleholder steady after much of it is covered with wet epoxy is also difficult. So stay on the safe side. Work on one area at a time. Let it dry overnight and then add more glass. When the base is completely covered with beach glass, finish the top by covering the top edge as well as about a half-inch of the inside with epoxy. Use the toothpick to smooth the epoxy, or to add texture by making tiny lines in it.

Clean any tools that you aren't going to throw away. Your knife does not have to be completely cleaned, but it will work best if you don't leave a great amount of excess epoxy to build up. If you mixed the epoxy in small amounts, you can continue working until the mixture is used. Cover your knife with waxed paper so that the epoxy will not stick to anything else before it is dry. The waxed paper can be peeled off the knife when you want to use it again. Throw away the cardboard on which you mixed the epoxy, and use a new piece the next time you work on the project.

To finish your candleholder, put melted wax and a wick inside the jar to make your own candle, or buy a candle of the appropriate size to insert in your candleholder. If you are making a vase, just add flowers. If the beach glass in the finished candleholder looks a bit dull to you, wipe each piece with mineral oil to deepen the color and add a sheen.

SAND CANDLES

Sand candles are nothing more than candles with a coating of sand, and they're fun to make.

First choose a container for your candle—the shape of your container will determine the shape of your finished candle. A short, fairly wide container will be easier to work with than a tall, narrow one. Press damp (not wet) sand all around the sides of the container. Then fill with melted wax and add a wick. You can purchase wax from a craft shop, but if you want to experiment first without using good supplies and have anumber of candle nubs, recycle them by melting them down and using the wax for your new candle.

When the wax is hard and cool to the touch, carefully remove the candle from the container and brush off any loose sand. Then, if you wish to make it more durable, spray the outside of the candle with a clear acrylic spray.

SHELL OR GLASS CANDLES

If you're already involved in making candles, consider adding embedded shells or beach glass for a different effect. Use a plain candleholder for your finished candle so that the candle itself rather than the holder is spotlighted.

One example of a sand candle

CHAPTER 7

SEA LOVERS' LAMPS

If you love the sea, you'll love a lamp made from sea treasures. The easiest lamps to make come all ready for you to fill with shells or beach glass. But you can also make interesting lamps from driftwood, or lobster buoys, or you can make a stunning beach glass lamp which resembles stained glass.

FILLED WITH SHELLS OR BEACH GLASS

Do you have a large collection of shells or beach glass? You can purchase a lamp which is constructed so that you can put your sea treasures into the clear glass base.

These lamps, all wired and complete with shades, can be found in many department or discount stores. If you can't find one in your area, Hilo Steiner (507 Broad Street, Shrewsbury, NJ 07701; 201-741-5862) of-

This lamp base has been filled with beach glass, but shells could be used instead

A Driftwood lamp. A plywood base for the driftwood would make it more stable

fers them my mail in a variety of shapes and sizes, from large table lamps to smaller bedside lamps. All these lamps include real shell finials. Send for a catalog.

Another possibility is to make your own lamp by purchasing a lamp fitting attached to a cork which will fit the top of a glass jug. These should be available in your local hardware store. Scout yard and garage sales for a good jug to use as the base if you don't have one already.

WITH DRIFTWOOD AND LOBSTER BUOYS

First you need a sturdy and attractive piece of driftwood or a lobster buoy to use as a lamp base. If your driftwood or buoy will not support itself and a lamp shade, you may secure the driftwood or buoy to a flat board to stabilize the base. A weathered board will look fine as is. A new board may be stained or antiqued to match the driftwood or lobster buoy. You can even use a broken buoy for a lamp. I made a small night lamp using only the top half of a buoy which split in two. I laid the half-buoy on its side so the broken part is on the bottom and doesn't show.

74

How To Attach Fittings For A Driftwood Lamp

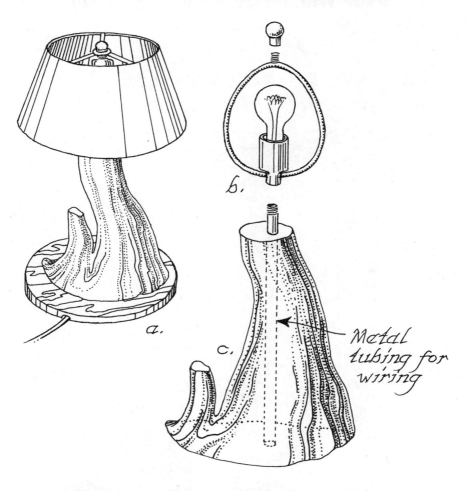

a.

b.

c.

Metal
tubing for
wiring

The wiring for the lamp may be added in two ways, depending upon the size of your finished lamp and the type of shade you desire. At the hardware store you can purchase wiring designed to fit a bottle. It is attached to a cork which you would insert into the bottle. You may use this type of wiring for a small lamp. Drill or carve a hole in the driftwood or buoy just large enough to hold the cork. Glue the cork into the hole with epoxy. When the epoxy is completely dry, add a light bulb and shade which clips onto the bulb, and your lamp is ready to use. Since the lamp is small, it will probably be useful only as a night light or for decoration.

If you want a larger lamp to use as a table lamp, you'll need one with separate hardware for the shade (electrical supply stores call this a "harp") so that it is not attached to the bulb. The hardware store can sup-

How To Attach Fittings For A Hanging Lamp
Made With Beach Glass And Epoxy

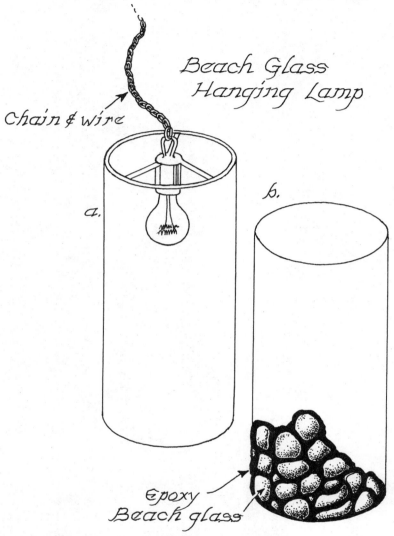

Beach Glass Hanging Lamp

Chain & wire

a.

b.

Epoxy Beach glass

ply wiring which goes through a narrow metal cylinder onto which you attach the fittings for the shade. The shade is then set on the top and held in place by a tightly screwed finial. To attach this type of wiring to your driftwood or buoy, you must drill a hole all the way through your base. Insert the metal cylinder containing the wiring into the hole you have drilled, and attach additional hardware for the shade at the top. If your driftwood is not very stable by itself, be sure to secure the driftwood to a flat board for added support before you insert the metal cylinder. To finish your lamp, screw in a light bulb and attach a shade. Your new lamp is all set to plug in.

MADE WITH BEACH GLASS—RESEMBLING STAINED GLASS

These beach glass lamps are especially beautiful because light shining through the beach glass brings out colors in an unusual way. The lamps are made by gluing beach glass to a fiberglass, glass, or plastic base. The finished lamp resembles one made from stained glass because the epoxy used around the edges of the beach glass pieces to glue them to the base is almost the color of lead. The beach glass is attached to the base in the same manner described in Chapter 6 for the candleholder.

After you have collected plenty of beach glass, you can locate a lamp base. It is important to have everything you need for a finished, working lamp **before** you begin attaching the beach glass. If you're lucky, you may find the whole lamp in one place. If not, you may find the base in one store, and then have to get fittings and electrical hardware in another.

Small lamp made from broken lobster buoy. Damaged part is on the bottom

Don't despair. Your finished lamp will be so beautiful, it will be worth all the trouble!

You can buy white plastic lamp bases, shaped as cylinders or globes, to which you must add wiring and chain so that the finished lamp can be hung as a swag lamp. You can purchase a swag lamp kit which includes everything but the base in a hardware, electrical supply, or craft store or buy wiring, lamp fittings, and chain separately.

Some lamps which can be covered with beach glass are sold as finished lamps. One style, sometimes called a cube table lamp, consists of a glass globe on a molded plastic base. A light fixture which can be used as a base for a beach glass lamp is a contemporary white globe which hangs directly from the ceiling. However, this fixture could be modified to hang as swag lamp although it would be beautiful covered with colored glass as it is. The old-fashioned hurricane lamp (electric or gas) is yet another style which can be changed dramatically when covered with beach glass.

If you are unable to find a ready-made base, you may have either a globe or cylinder molded from clear fiberglass. Keep in mind that the finished lamp will be the same shape as the base you start with but covered

Beach glass lamp in progress. Small pieces
of beach glass are attached with epoxy

Hanging lamp made with
beach glass and epoxy

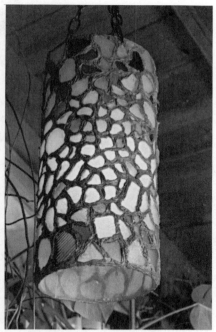

Another beach glass and epoxy lamp

Finished hanging lamp made
from beach glass and epoxy

with colored pieces of glass. Any lamp style which can be covered in this way can be used. Even the old standard pole lamp would look great after beach glass covers the plastic shades and transforms the lamp into something really different and special.

If your lamp base, globe or cylinder, doesn't already include wiring, take it to the hardware or electrical supply store where you can get the electrical hardware; socket, plug, wire, and chain for hanging, if desired. The lamp hardware may require small holes in the top of the base for attaching the socket or chain. Ready-made bases may already have the holes, especially if they are part of a lamp kit. If not, you will have to get the electrical fittings, determine where holes are needed, have them drilled, and then make sure you leave these holes clear when you attach the beach glass to your lamp base.

Once you're sure how your finished lamp will operate, check it over to see where you will attach beach glass. Your light bulb must remain accessible, so don't glue the globe itself to the base if it must be lifted to reach the bulb! After the epoxy dries, the attachment is permanent.

Also make sure you have more beach glass than you need to cover the lamp where the light will shine through. You need a variety of sizes, shapes, and colors since gluing the pieces of glass on the lamp is something like doing a jigsaw puzzle. If one piece won't fit, another will. Small spaces can be filled with epoxy if you don't have a piece of glass the size and shape you need.

In addition to the lamp and plenty of beach glass, gather the following materials: epoxy (black and gray in paste form; the brand name PC-7 is available from building supplies and hardware stores), cotton swabs, acetone or epoxy thinner, an old knife, a piece of cardboard on which to mix the epoxy, plenty of sturdy toothpicks (try cocktail toothpicks), and a couple of rags.

To attach the beach glass, read and follow the directions given in Chapter 6 for making the candleholder which resembles stained glass.

When you have completely covered the base with beach glass, finish any raw edge by coating it with epoxy. Again, make sure you don't glue shut your only access to the light blub! When the epoxy is dry, your globe or cylinder can be wired and hung. Both globes and cylinders make very attractive swag lamps which can be hung from black or gold chain. If you've used another style lamp as a base, just add a bulb and plug it in.

People will notice and admire your completed lamp, and you'll be pleased and proud to tell them you made it yourself. You may also find yourself swamped with requests from friends and relatives who want lamps for themselves. You can tell them how easily they can make their own, or surprise them with a special holiday or birthday gift, or use this opportunity to make a few extra dollars by starting your own lamp business!

This mobile mixes driftwood,
shells and sea animals

John Ross used only driftwood
to make this tiny mobile

CHAPTER 8

MOBILES AND WIND CHIMES FOR OLD SALTS

Mobiles and wind chimes captivate the eye and ear, and they're easy to make.

MOBILES

There are several different ways you can make a mobile from which to hang your sea treasures. You can display any lightweight items, such as shells, small pieces of driftwood, beach glass, sand dollars, crab claws, or starfish.

Mobiles Using Wire from Coat Hangers as Branches

The easiest mobile to make has only two branches from which you can hang four items. Get two wire coat hangers. Using wire cutters, cut off the longest pieces of the coat hangers to use for your mobile base. Use pliers to bend both tips on both pieces into hooks to hold the lines from which you'll hang your shells or small pieces of driftwood.

Make a cross from the two pieces of wire and tie them together with transparent thread or fishing line (more durable than thread). Dab some glue on the knot to make sure it stays in place.

Make a loop from another piece of thread or line and tie it to the intersection of the two wire branches so that you can hang your mobile. Dab glue on these knots, too.

Select the shells or pieces of driftwood you want to hang on your mobile. Drill holes in them. Use transparent thread or fishing line to hang them from the tips of the wire branches, one at each end of each wire branch.

Test the balance of the mobile by hanging it up and shortening or lengthening the lines as needed. When you have the balance right on each branch and have tied knots in your lines, dab glue on all the knots to make sure they don't come undone. When the glue is dry, your mobile is ready to hang.

Mobile Using Driftwood as Branches

You can make a more interesting mobile using several pieces of driftwood instead of coat hanger wire for the branches. You'll also need a spool of lightweight wire if you want to hang beach glass and don't have a special bit for drilling holes in glass.

Find a place where you can hang the mobile as you are working on it. The corner of a door or a hook for a hanging plant will work. The top part of your mobile should be the longest and heaviest of your driftwood branches. Drill three or more holes through the wood: one in the middle for hanging the mobile, and as many more as you need to hang the other pieces of wood you plan to use. Estimate where on the main piece these latter holes should be placed so that your mobile will balance when you attach the secondary pieces of wood. One good plan for a mobile is one long branch with three smaller ones hanging from the main one. If your driftwood is too fragile or you don't have a drill, you can purchase small screw eyes from the hardware store, and hang the other pieces from them.

Using the transparent line, make one loop through the middle hole in the biggest piece for hanging your mobile. Then, use the other holes to attach the other wood pieces to the main pieces with the transparent line. Now hang the mobile on a corner of a door as you add the other hanging pieces. You will have to keep lifting the top loop off the door to check your mobile for balance. Shortening or lengthening the line holding the hanging items is one way to redistribute the weight. Another way is to substitute a lighter shell or piece of glass for a heavier one or vice-versa.

Holes can be drilled through shells, sand dollars, and the like so that they can be hung from the secondary wood pieces. You can't, however, drill a hole through beach glass with an ordinary drill bit. If you don't have a bit for drilling glass and don't wish to purchase one, you can enclose the glass in thin wire, tying a small loop at one end from which to hang it, or glue the transparent line directly to the glass. Use epoxy to make sure it stays glued. Some pieces of beach glass are shaped so that transparent line can be wrapped around and tied without its slipping off. You'll have to do some experimenting to find the best ways to hang the beach glass.

Check to see how your finished mobile will hang by taking the top loop in your hand and holding it so that the mobile hangs freely. Make any adjustments necessary to improve the balance. If you don't plan to hang your mobile immediately, be careful to store it so that its lines don't get all tangled. One solution for this problem is to carefully put each unit of the mobile loosely into its own plastic bag.

Table-Top Mobile

Claude Bonang, creator of the starfish people in Chapter 10, makes small mobiles which can sit on a desk or table top instead of being hung.

Find a sturdy scallop, quahog, or other fairly flat shell to serve as the base. Drill a hole in the middle of the shell toward the back. Then cut a piece of wire about 7 inches long. A piece from a coat hanger will do. Bend the wire to look like a comma. On the tip of the comma, bend the edge around to form a hook from which you can hang the branches of your mobile. Stand the other end of the wire comma in the hole of your shell base and then use epoxy to glue the wire in place. If needed for stability, add lead weights under the shell base.

Cut two more pieces of wire to use as branches and tie them together in the manner described above for the hanging mobile made from coat

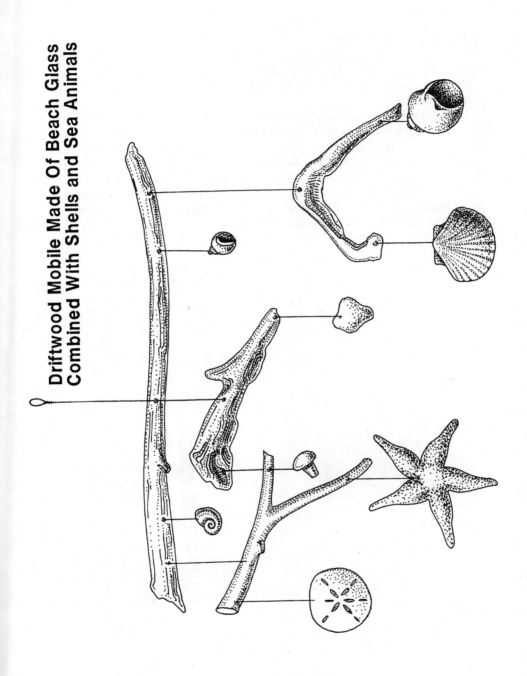

hangers. Then follow the rest of the directions there. Your finished mobile will be smaller, but made the same way as the other coat hanger
mobil.

Other Ideas for Mobiles

For a mobile which moves more freely, get a small swivel hook from the hardware store. Suspend the main branch or branches of the mobile from the swivel hook and also use the hook to attach the hanging loop of the mobile.

Mobiles can contain anything that you find interesting or attractive. Because the shapes and weight of your driftwood as well as the other sea treasures you use will vary, each mobile you make will be unique. You can, for example, make a mobile entirely of driftwood if you so choose. Jon Ross, who also makes the shell animals described in Chapter 10, made one small mobile all from tiny pieces of driftwood. He made another by hanging several small whales he carved from wood. Use your imagination to see what you can come up with.

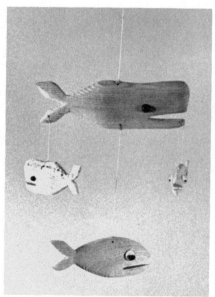

Mobile by John Ross displays wood whales that he carved from driftwood. Eyes were purchased in a crafts store

Wind chime from Tonga in the South Pacific, made from shells and seed pods. "Chimes" are spines of a large sea urchin.

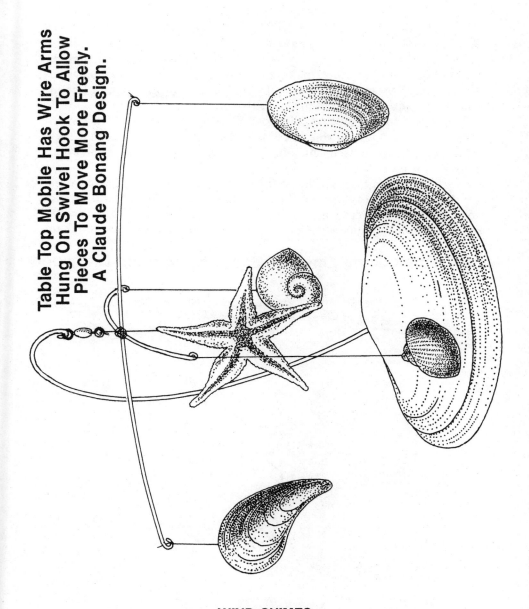

Table Top Mobile Has Wire Arms Hung On Swivel Hook To Allow Pieces To Move More Freely. A Claude Bonang Design.

WIND CHIMES

Unlike mobiles, shell wind chimes do not have to achieve a delicate balance. Thus, they are somewhat easier to make than mobiles. The basic wind chime is simply a branch-like piece of driftwood, or other base, from which several rows of shells hang.

Choose a piece of driftwood to use for the base, and shells to hang in rows from the driftwood. Estimate how many rows you will need to make the wind chime even. Scallop shells, if you can find enough, are excellent, but several varieties of shells will work. Jingle shells make a lovely sound! Drill holes in the tops of all the shells and then use transparent line to hook them together, making the rows to hang. Tie knots between shells to keep them from slipping. Leave some extra transparent line at the top of each row to tie it to the driftwood.

Remember to dab glue on all knots made in plastic line or thread so they don't come loose. If you don't have transparent line or thread, heavy black thread can be used. The black thread will almost disappear when looked at from a distance.

Next drill holes through the driftwood (or substitute small screw eyes for the holes) to hold the rows of shells you will hang. You should lay the rows of shells and the base on a flat surface first to determine exactly where the holes should be drilled. The shells should hang close enough to

Wind Chimes Using Lines Of Shells Hung From Driftwood

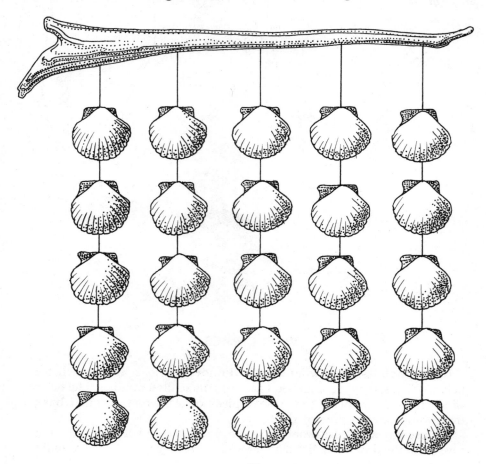

each other so that they will touch when the wind blows. Also drill a hole in the center of the base so you can make a loop for hanging the finished wind chime.

Wind chimes and mobiles can be made without a driftwood base. One substitute is a large, fairly flat shell. Another is the top of a metal can. In either case, drill holes around the edges for the rows of shells to chime and two in the middle through which you will add a hook or line to hang the finished piece. Then glue tiny shells or crushed shells all over the top and bottom of the can top, but leave the holes you drilled open so that you can attach the rows of chimes. Make as many hanging rows of shells as you need by drilling holes in the shells and stringing them on transparent line. Tie knots between shells so they won't slip. Tie these strings of shells to the base and hang your finished piece where it will catch a breeze.

If you don't have access to a drill, you can use a small basket turned upsidedown as a base for a wind chime. Thread the line from which you hang your shells through the holes in the basket weave.

Don't be afraid to experiment with different kinds of shells for your wind chime. You can mix varieties rather than trying to use shells of only one type. Be sure to put only tough shells on a wind chime which will hang where the wind is strong. More delicate shells can be used on a wind chime for a more sheltered area. Even if you don't hear your shells chime often or even at all, they will still be wonderful to see.

Wind Chimes Using Metal Or Plastic Cover To Hang Strings of Shells In a Circle

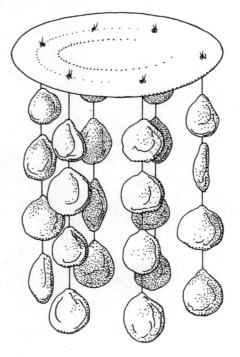

CHAPTER 9

BEACHCOMBER'S JEWELRY

Until you see them sparkle in the light, you can't image how beautiful beach glass earrings are. You can create a whole collection of beachcomber's jewelry using beach glass, shells, and some imagination.

MAKING NECKLACES FROM SHELLS

Try a shell necklace. Find your prettiest shells. Mix different kinds and sizes of shells together or match them and make a strand using all small periwinkle shells, for example. Drill a hole in each shell and then string them on transparent line. Tie a knot after each shell you add, so the shells won't all fall off if the necklace breaks.

You can make several strands of different lengths to wear together or separately. Make one strand with white shells, another with shells of dark colors, and a third mixing light and dark shades.

Consider mixing shells with wooden beads or seeds. If you have a special shell, make a necklace chain from small shells and hang your treasured shell as a pendant in the center.

Shell necklaces. Seed pods have been mixed with shells in center necklace

Single-stone beach glass pendants and earrings. The larger pendant
(top right) is made from several chips of beach glass

AN EASY WAY USING RECYCLED JEWELRY

Here's an easy way to make your old jewelry look new or create something really special from jewelry you can buy, often for less than a dollar. Beach glass and tiny shells can be used to make tie tacks, earrings, pendants, sweater guards, and rings.

Attach the glass or shells to the jewelry base with clear glue. Make sure the glue is not water soluable. Epoxy is probably best. You'll get a better bond if you mix wisps of cotton with the glue. A piece of beach glass can be used individually like a precious stone, or several chips can be put together for a different effect.

If you have an old ring which is missing a stone or earrings that you think are too plain, you can rejuvenate them with beach glass. What an easy way to change earrings you're tired of for some which are new and certainly different!

Search the jewelry counter in a dime store, or buy more expensive pieces in a jewelry store. You're looking for tie tacks, earrings, pendants, or rings that are plain and could be dressed up with beach glass added.

I've found several good pairs of earrings in the "closeout bin" for almost nothing. What you have to look for is a style that has a smooth, fairly flat surface to which you can glue the shells or glass.

You can make a matching set of earrings and pendant by finding three pieces of glass of the same color and similar shapes, but you need a fairly large collection of very small and well-polished glass in order to find two pieces for the earrings plus another one for the pendant.

Look through all your pieces to find matching pieces for earrings. It's not as difficult as you might imagine to find two or three pieces of the same size, shape, and color. Remember they don't have to match perfectly since no one looks closely at two earrings at once when someone is wearing them. Besides, part of the appeal of handcrafted items is that no two are exactly alike. Each piece of beach glass, like a snow flake, is unique.

I made one ring by scraping some imitation stones off a cheap ring and replacing them with tiny chips of blue beach glass. The ring no longer looks cheap! Another ring I have is of higher quality. I purchased a hand-made ring of sterling silver with an open diamond design, just the right size to hold an almost heart-shaped piece of beach glass. Everyone who sees the ring askes what the "stone" is!

The pendant made with several chips of different colored beach glass could be done instead with shell chips.

The suncatchers described in Chapter 11 also make beautiful pendants just by being hung on a rope or chain.

Bracelets can be made in the same manner. Glue beach glass to plain links or hang a stone from a chain.

MAKING JEWELRY FROM SCRATCH

If you're more ambitious, you can buy fittings for making earrings and necklaces. Then, using beach glass or shells, make your own jewelry from scratch by gluing beach glass or shells to bell caps, earring fittings, or fili-gree. You can find everything you need for earrings, pendants, and the like in your local craft shop.

Once you begin making your own jewelry, you'll invent some wonderful creations. One thing you can be sure of. No one else will have anything just like yours.

Beach glass rings. The largest one is made with several tiny chips of glass instead of a single polished piece

CHAPTER 10

SEA-BORN CREATURES PEOPLE AND PETS

You can have fun making starfish, shells, or rocks into clever little people and pets. Experiment with the things you've picked up on the beach and have around the house to create animals and creatures other than the ones described here.

STARFISH PEOPLE

These clever starfish people are the creation of a former high school biology teacher. Using his imagination and depending primarily on raw materials gathered from the sea, Claude Bonag shapes starfish into different poses, and by decorating and dressing them up a bit, makes them look like cheerleaders, tennis players, golfers, and warriors.

To make these people, you must have living starfish because once they've dried out, you can't change their shapes. If you already have some dried starfish, however, perhaps you can see a "person" in the way they've already posed.

Considering that the five arms of the starfish can be thought of as a head, two arms, and two legs of a person, decide what kind of person you want to make and the pose that will be required. A cheerleader, for exam-

Starfish gladiator (sand dollar shield,
nail sword, and crab victim)

Starfish cheerleader with
crepe paper pompons

91

Starfish people

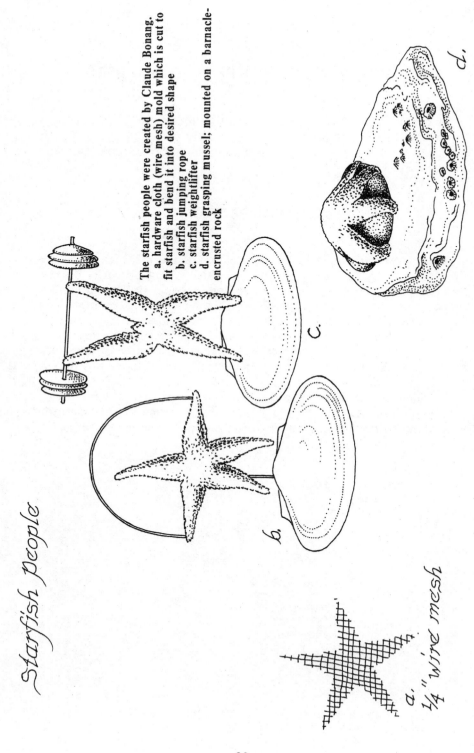

The starfish people were created by Claude Bonang.
a. hardware cloth (wire mesh) mold which is cut to
fit starfish and bend it into desired shape
b. starfish jumping rope
c. starfish weightlifter
d. starfish grasping mussel; mounted on a barnacle-
encrusted rock

a. ¼" wire mesh

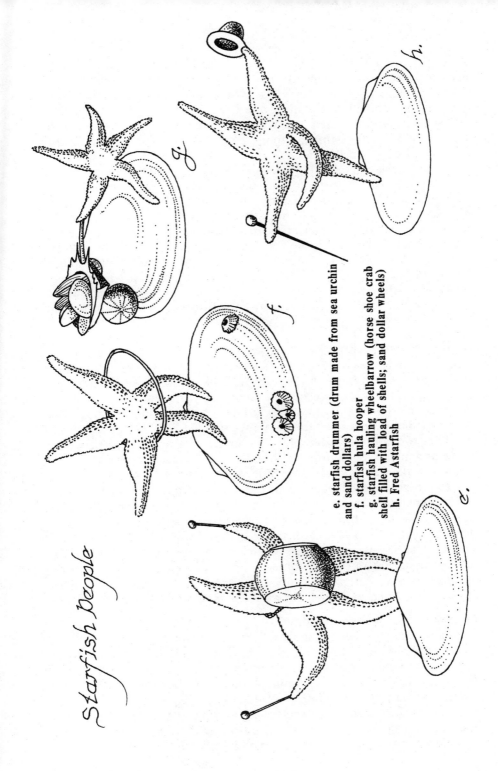

Starfish people

e. starfish drummer (drum made from sea urchin and sand dollars)
f. starfish hula hooper
g. starfish hauling wheelbarrow (horse shoe crab shell filled with load of shells; sand dollar wheels)
h. Fred Astarfish

93

ple, might have her arms in the air and one leg kicking up. One arm of the starfish then will be the cheerleader's head; two arms, the cheerleader's arms; and the last two arms, her legs. When the starfish is dried in the appropriate pose, glue it to a scallop, or other appropriately shaped shell, or driftwood mounting. Then add whatever else you want. For the cheerleader, you'd make two tiny pompoms from crepe paper and glue them to the ends of both arms.

Similarly, you can make the starfish into many other types of people by creating the right position for the body and adding the right accouterments. Experiment. Your imagination is the only limit to how many different starfish people you can create. A student starfish might be sitting down, leaning against a tiny driftwood tree, head bent over reading a tiny book. Use other items in your beachcombing collection as well. For instance, Claude Bonang designed a starfish warrior who proudly points his sword (a nail) and a sand dollar shield at the victim beside him, a small crab. All were glued on a scallop shell. Another is hauling a wagon filled with mussels. The wagon is an upsidedown horse shoe crab with sand dollar wheels.

Getting the Starfish in the Right Position

In order to get the starfish dried in the right shape, you must shape the starfish and soak it in a solution of 95% sea water and 5% formaldehyde. If you put a living starfish into the solution before "putting it to sleep," however, the shock may cause it to lose an arm or curl up so tightly that you can't shape it. So use either a syringe or a medicine dropper to insert a drop or two of the soaking solution into the starfish's mouth (the center of the underside). Then drop the starfish into a bucket or other container filled with the soaking solution while you get your forms ready.

Use hardware cloth to make your forms. This is quarter-inch wire mesh which you can purchase in a hardware store. Cut the cloth into the shape of a starfish about the same size as the starfish you are working with. Then bend the hardware cloth into the shape you want for the starfish people. The cheerleader would be straight except for one raised "leg." Take your starfish out of the solution and put it against the mold, bending it to fit. Wrap the starfish and mold in ace bandages or strips of sheeting material. Then soak again for a day, remove, and dry in the bandages.

Finishing the Starfish Person

Remove the bandages. If the starfish isn't completely dry, let it sit out and air dry until it is. Insert a wire in the leg or both legs, if two legs will be touching the base on which the starfish will be mounted. Then, to protect it, dip the starfish in polyurethane or spray with clear acrylic. When the finish coat is dry, drill hole(s) in the appropriate places on your scallop shell or driftwood base, insert the legs of the starfish, and glue with epoxy. Cover the bottom of the base by gluing a piece of felt on it. Your starfish person is now ready to dress and decorate as needed.

94

Considering their hobbies and special interests, you can surprise your friends with just the right starfish people.

ROCK PETS AND PEOPLE WATCHERS

Do you like little animals? Why buy a pet rock when you can make your own?

Paint faces on rocks and make them into "pets." Or add a caption. A rock with a painted sleeping face might be labeled "I never get up on Monday!" One clever gift shop creation is nothing more than a big rock to which little rocks with painted faces have been glued. The humor comes from its title, "Rock Concert."

Jon Ross's People Watchers are similar to the "Rock Concert" except that they can be made of many different materials either alone or in combination: wood, rocks, shells, beach glass, or lobster shell pieces. The pieces of materials become people once they have had craft store moveable eyes glued on. Grouped together as if posing for a photograph, they stand mounted with glue to a small flat piece of driftwood. Jon Ross's other name for these people groups is "Family Portrait."

Jon Ross has also created several animals using rocks and other materials.

The Owl has a rock body, small mussel-shell wings, uncooked kernels of popcorn (or tiny yellow periwinkle shells) for his beak and feet, brown periwinkle-shell ears, painted feathers on his chest, and craft store

Jon Ross's people watchers.
This one's all driftwood

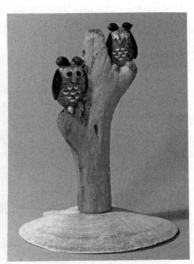

Jon Ross's owls perched
in driftwood "tree"

Jon Ross's owl

moveable eyes. The owls can be glued on driftwood as if they were perching on a tree or mounted to a scallop shell, or other shell base.

The Dog is a dachshund who has a long rock for his body, periwinkle-shell head with painted on eyes and nose, mussel-shell ears, periwinkle-shell feet, and a glued-on felt tail.

Jon Ross used lobster shell parts for these people watchers

These people watchers are a mixture of shells,
beach glass, and driftwood (a Jon Ross creation)

Penguins have oval-shaped rock bodies, some of which were naturally white for the penguins' stomachs. In cases where the rock isn't white in that area, Jon paints it white. The penguins have mussel-shell wings, tiny mussel-shell feet, dark-colored periwinkle-shell heads, painted-on noses with yellow tips, and glued-on craft store eyes. The finished penguins are glued to a flat driftwood base.

ANIMAL MAGNETS

Want to make little shell animal magnets? Here are two ideas. You can create others.

Owl

For the owl you need a large pine cone chip for the body, a wooden matchstick for the perch, a pair of very small clam shells for the wings,

Jon Ross's dachshund

Jon Ross's penguins

three tiny shells or shell chips for the beak and feet, and eyes. You can buy white plastic eyes with moveable black irises in a craft store. Glue the parts to the pine cone chip according to the illustration. When the glue on your owl is dry, glue a magnet to its back. In the craft store you will find plastic-coated magnets in strips which can easily be cut to size. A cute and clever owl is ready to perch on your refrigerator door.

Mouse

The shell mouse requires one shell for the body—a periwinkle or snail will do—thin wire for the whishers and tail; and tiny black plastic rings (available from a craft store) for the eyes and nose. You can substitute something similar for the eyes and nose or paint them on the shell with black paint.

Look at the illustration as you glue the parts together. Cut several short strands of wire for the tail and glue to the bottom of the shell so that the tail sticks out the thin end of the shell. The magnet can be glued on top of the wire. Then cut several more strands of wire for the whiskers. Run the wires through the tiny black plastic ring (nose) and glue to the front tip of the fat end of the shell. If you don't have the ring, just glue wire to the shell and paint the nose on. Add the eyes by gluing on two more black plastic rings or paint them on.

When he's dry, this cute little sea mouse will happily join the own on your refrigerator door.

Jon Ross makes his shell mice a little differently and mounts them on small pieces of wood, but they could be made as magnets. His periwinkle mouse has a tail cut from an elastic band and painted nose with no whiskers. By mounting two mice, nose to nose, Jon Ross makes a pair of kissing mice. But two single magnet mice could fall in love and kiss on any refrigerator door!

MORE ANIMALS TO MAKE

You can make many kinds of animals from shells to stand alone. The mouse doesn't have to be a magnet but can instead be mounted on driftwood or sit by itself on a whatnot shelf.

"Kissing mice," by Jon Ross.
Could also be used as a refrigerator magnet

In addition to a variety of shells, you may also need the following materials to make shell animals—all available in your local craft shop: eyes, felt, pipe cleaners or bump chenille, and then wire. You probably have around the house other items that you might want to use in some ani-

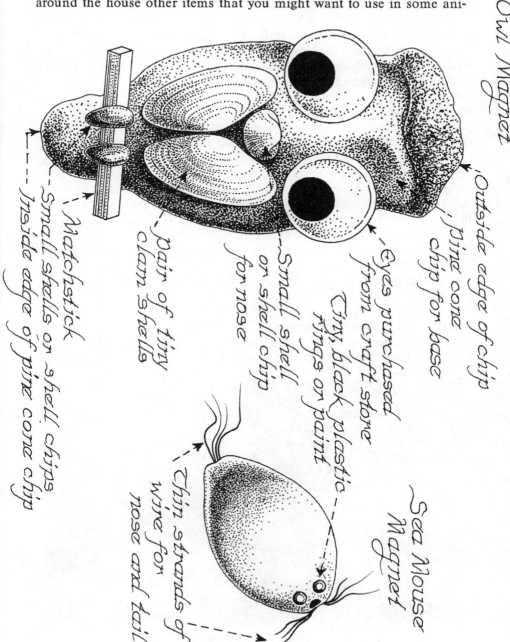

Owl Magnet

Outside edge of chip

Pine cone chip for base

Eyes purchased from craft store

Tiny, black plastic rings or paint

Small shell or shell chip for nose

Pair of tiny clam shells

Matchstick

Small shells or shell chips

Inside edge of pine cone chip

Sea Mouse Magnet

Thin strands of wire for nose and tail

mals, such as bristles from a brush for whiskers. You'll have to pick up your own shells on the beach although if you can't get beachcombing anytime soon, you may be able to order some by mail. Some craft shops sell shells. Check the one nearest you.

Although some shellcraft books specify that certain shells are needed to make certain animals, you really don't need special shells to make most animals because the way you can tell one animal from another has more to do with its features, such as ears, tail, and whiskers than its general shape. Here's one example to show you what I mean.

Pine Cone and Shell Animals

Take a medium-sized pine cone. Glue two eyes on it and attach two small shells at the bottom for feet. What is it? An owl, of course.

Take the same pine cone. Glue two eyes on it. Bend about a four-inch length of bump chanille in half and twist to look like rabbit ears and glue them to the pine cone, one on each side near the top and toward the back. Add two small shells at the bottom for feet and a small pompon or cotton ball on the back for tail. What you have this time is a pine cone bunny.

You can also make a cat in much the same way. If you have shells in the shape of cat's ears, use them. If not, cut small triangles from felt and glue them to the pine cone.

Consider turning the pine cone on its side and adding four feet instead of two.

Making Eyeglasses for Animals

You can put spectacles on any shell animal you make if you have some thin wire. Bend the wire into the shape of old-fashioned granny glasses

Turtle by Jon Ross

100

and put them on your animal with the eyes peeking through, and glue them in place. If you want to add glasses to a pine cone animal, you can hook them into the pine cone without glue.

Mice

You can make mice with a variety of shells. With cockle shells, a large cockle shell becomes the body, with two small cockle shells as ears. Add small shells for feet and eyes. Add wire or brush bristle whiskers, and make a tail from pipe cleaner or wire.

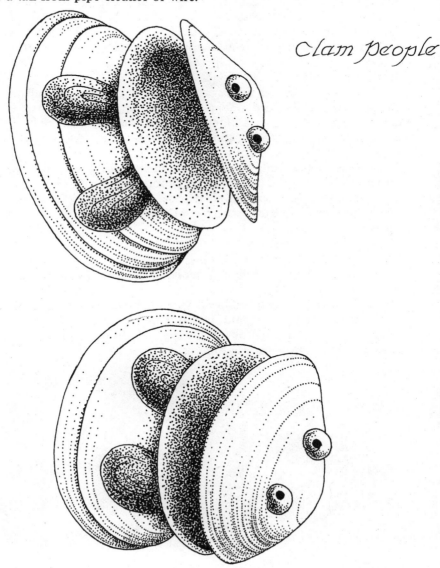

Clam people

A small snail or tulip shell, mounted on its side on a piece of driftwood, or a flat shell can also be a mouse. Use shell chips or very tiny shells—any kind—for ears and feet. You don't really need feet to get a mouse effect. Add eyes, whiskers, and tail, as you did for the cockle shell mouse above.

Bunny or Cat
Glue two fairly good-sized cockle shells together for the body and mount on driftwood or on a flat shell. Glue another cockle shell, a little smaller than the body shells, across the front of the body for the head. Add long ears of bump chanille or felt if you want a bunny or shorter, traingular shaped ears for a cat. Glue eyes, appropriate tails, and whiskers.

Turtle
What could be easier than making a turtle? With tiny shells or shell chips for its four feet and tail, and a slightly larger shell for its head, you can make a turtle out of a clam, cockle, or quahog shell. Put the body parts in the appropriate locations, add eyes, and glue to a driftwood or shell mount.

Jon Ross's water turtle has a sea urchin shell for a body, mussel shells for feet and tail, and a periwinkle shell for a head with painted-on eyes. He is mounted on a scallop shell base. Jon's land turtle or tortoise is made the same way except the feet aremade with periwinkle instead of mussel shells.

Frog or Clam Person
Glue two halves of large clam or quahog shells together so that it is open ¼ to ½ inch on the unhinged side. That space becames the frog's mouth. You can match halves of different kinds of shells if you don't have two half clam shells. Glue or paint two eyes to the top shell, the frog's head. Mount on a scallop shell or small piece of driftwood. Add wire granny glasses if you want your frog to look studious.

Seal by Jon Ross   Frog by Jon Ross

Jon Ross's frog has a sea urchin shell body with a smaller sea urchin shell head. The eyes are painted on tiny periwinkle shells which have been glued to the head. The frogs' feet are sea urchin chips. He's mounted on a scallop shell base.

Seal

Jon Ross's seal has a periwinkle body, slightly smaller periwinkle head with painted-on eyes and nose, and tiny mussel shell feet. The seal is glued to a rock base to simulate the natural rocks in the bay on which seals often sun themselves.

Skunk

To make a skunk, Jon Ross uses different-sized periwinkle shells for the body, head, and feet. For the tail, he then adds a mussel shell with both halves still together. Then he paints the skunk's eyes, nose, and a white stripe from his head to his tail.

Raccoon

Jon Ross makes the raccoon in the same way as the skunk with different sizes of dark-colored periwinkle shells. He paints on the eyes, yellow in center fringed with white and then black. Then he paints on the nose, and rings around the tail. The tail is a complete mussel shell with both halves intact.

Porcupine

Jon Ross's porcupine has half a sea urchin shell (spines intact) glued side-down to a mussel shell base. His head is a periwinkle shell with painted nose, and glued-on craft store eyes. The tail is a tiny mussel shell glued to the base.

Other Animal Ideas To Consider

Besides the animals mentioned here, you can also make these animals

Skunk by Jon Ross

from differing combinations of the shells you've picked up on the beach. For example, a squirrel can be several pieces of bump chenille wound together for a bushy tail. For a bird, attach some feathers. Make lobster claws from red bump chanille. A crab can have pipe cleaner legs. You can make a monkey, dog, penguin, pelican, or turkey, to name just a few.

And then, of course, you can create a mythical animal, an animal that exists only because you made it. Just as many of the animals we read about in myths and legends never existed, your creature doesn't have to look like anything that really lives. Have fun. Be inventive with your shells.

LOBSTER SHELL PEOPLE

Jon Ross creates many different people using the shells of lobsters that have already been cooked and eaten, a way to recycle garbage!

Jon first carefully washes the shells using a garden hose with the sprayer nozzle. Then he lets them dry outside. They'll smell terrible, he warns, if you don't get all the meat out.

Since the sun-drying bleaches much of the red color out, he re-colors them before using them in crafts. Using the same kind of red or orange dye you would use to dye cloth, he soaks them in a dye bath. After the lobster shell pieces have been dyed and are completely dry, he uses them to make people.

Lobster Lady

The lobster lady is mounted on a scallop shell. Her head is a lobster claw. The feeler ends were glued on and then painted black to make her eyes. Her hair is lichen gathered from a spruce tree. Two lobster legs make her arms, and her skirt is created by gluing lobster tail pieces back-to-back. You could substitute straw or other material for the hair if you don't have lichen nearby.

Racoon by Jon Ross

The Old Salt Lobster Standing

The Old Salt stands on a scallop shell base. The main part of the lobster body forms his back. His chest and stomach are created from lobster tail pieces. His head, like the lady's, is a lobster claw. His eyes are glued-on craft store eyes instead of lobster feelers. Lobster shell legs make his arms. His legs are the small ends of the lobster claws. His boots are pieces from the lobster's tail. The familiar yellow storm gear hat is cut from a roll of yellow shelf paper. His pipe is made from two sizes of dowels cut to size and glued.

The Old Salt Lobster Resting

This tired old lobster person reclines on a driftwood bed. He, too, has a lobster claw head and lobster body stomach. His legs are made from the tops of the lobster claws with tail pieces for his boots. He has lobster feeler tips glued on and painted black for eyes like the lady lobster and a shelf-paper hat and dowel pipe like the other old salt.

●

These are just some ideas for making a variety of animals and people from rocks, shells, and other materials you can pick up on or near the beach or scavenge from trash. Use your imagination to create others.

Jon Ross's Lobster Lady   **Old Salt Lobster by Jon Ross**

CHAPTER 11

SEA CRAFTS USING DRIFTWOOD, SHELLS, SEA GLASS AND SAND

Many simple crafts can be made from your sea treasures. Some of useful in a study, while others are just fun to make and have. Wall hangings or collages for decoration, bulletin boards, pencil holders, book ends, night lights, and magnets can all remind you of your sunny afternoons on the beach. Use your imagination to develop variations on the potpourri of crafts described here.

SIMPLE DRIFTWOOD DESIGNS

Many of the pieces of driftwood that you'll find will look like animals or smooth, silvery abstract sculptures. Use them as free-standing works of art or mount them on weathered, antiqued, or stained board and hang them on the wall. Create your own gallery by adding a small plaque with the title of your art work. The title you choose for your art can also let an unenlightened viewer know what to look for in your masterpiece.

Driftwood Art

Use your imagination when you find a piece of driftwood. If you find a smooth, silvery piece which resembles a seal, use the driftwood as a "sculpture." If you like the design and texture of a piece of wood but it doesn't look like anything, hang it above your fireplace mantelpiece as a free form wall sculpture. Notice how other people have used driftwood when you visit summer homes along the shore or drive along nearby roads.

You can create an abstract "painting" (actually a collage) from driftwood just be gluing or nailing (tiny nails, please!) an assortment of various sizes and shapes of smaller driftwood pieces to a plywood backing the size you want the finished piece to be.

Sign made from a single piece of driftwood

Driftwood Collage

Driftwood can be used as a background to highlight rocks, shells, and sea creatures. Mount a horseshoe crab or special shell on a flat piece of driftwood and mount on the wall. I found a beautiful little gray and white rock which, because of its shape and shading, looks like an Arab woman dressed in a galabaya and veil. I mounted the rock on driftwood and entitled the piece "The Arab Woman."

Driftwood Sign

Driftwood Signs

Do you need a sign for your house or the corner of your street? Find a fairly flat piece of driftwood which is the right size for your sign. Lightly pencil the lettering you want on the board.

Using a woodburning tool or an electric engraving tool (the kind you buy to mark keys or equipment), hollow out the lettering you have drawn on the driftwood. Keep going over the letters as many times as necessary to make deep grooves about ⅛ inch wide for all letters. If you wish, add a design, such as a seagull.

Then, find a small paintbrush (such as you might have from a watercolor paint set) and some outside latex house paint. White shows up best, but you can use any color. If your sign will not be outside, then you can use any kind of paint. Paint made to use inside the house will not weather the elements outdoors. Carefully fill in the lettering on your sign with the paint. You could make the sign just by painting the lettering on the board, but the engraved lettering will last longer and looks more professional. A rental company in a coastal town made its driftwood sign by hanging several weathered boards together to form a flat although irregular surface and then attaching ready-made white letters to spell out the company name.

Driftwood Drawings

If you have some talent in drawing, you can use a flat, weathered board as the base for a drawing. The weathered board is a great background for any drawing related to the sea. Sketch your drawing lightly in pencil.

Driftwood makes a good scratching post for cats. Tashka rests after a vigorous scratching session!

Then engrave the pencil lines as described above under "Driftwood Signs." Finally fill in the lines with paint. Don't forget to sign your work as the artist!

More Driftwood Ideas

Some driftwood may be already shaped to hold a plant pot. Set your favorite plant in the middle of the driftwood and place the arrangement on a table inside your house. Driftwood also makes a decorative support for a plant which needs assistance to stand up straight as it grows tall. Even if your plant doesn't need any support, driftwood placed as decoration with plants is very attractive. You can use driftwood this way inside your house or outdoors in a flower garden.

Driftwood can also be used as a base for dried floral arrangements. At Christmas the driftwood becomes a holiday centerpiece with red candles, evergreen boughs, and shiny Christmas ornaments. You can substitute a paper turkey and gold candles for Thanksgiving, or a bunny or chicks and white candles for Easter.

Weathered boards can be nailed together to form an attractive box in which to set plant pots, either inside your house, or outside on a deck or patio. Add some rope as trim around the top edges or lower as a band design.

Most cats like driftwood for sharpening their claws. Protect your upholstered furniture by putting a piece of weathered wood in your family

Cork bulletin board used as base for seacraft wall hanging

109

room for your pets. Don't choose your very favorite driftwood for this purpose, since the cats will do quite a job on it.

WALL HANGINGS, COLLAGES, AND BULLETIN BOARDS

Any weathered board makes a great base for a sea collage. Just glue shells, beach glass, or whatever in an arrangement which pleases your eye. You can even add sand and seaweed in places.

If you want a weathered board for a bulletin board and all the ones you've picked up on the beach are too small, get a piece of plywood for a backing, stain or antique the plywood to resemble driftwood. Using small nails, attach several smaller weathered boards to the plywood base to cover it. If you wish, decorate the edges with other beachcombing treasures. If you plan far enough ahead, you can "weather" your own board by leaving it outside for several months.

Instead of plywood for a backing, if you don't have any weathered board, purchase a cork bulletin board, or cover a board with burlap or sand. Once you have your background ready, glue on in an artistic arrangement, whatever you wish—shells, starfish, beach glass, sand dollars, and/or small crabs. If you use crabs, don't forget to varnish them or dip them in polyurethane first to preserve them. Drape fishnet around the edges or over the corners for extra emphasis. Hang the finished work on the wall like a painting.

A Connecticut artist, who has received a good deal of publicity for his work, uses only what he can pick up on the beach—driftwood, sand, shells, seaweed, etc. to create realistic reproductions of existing lighthouses and other miniature nautical scenes, such as docks complete with

Pencil holder with burlap covering   Pencil holder with sand covering

little dinghies and fish houses. When he first started, he tried selling driftwood with plants which nobody wanted. Now he has no trouble selling his work even though some pieces go for well over $100 each.

If you want to use the wall hanging as a bulletin board for your desk area rather than as a work of art, decorate only the edges with shells and starfish, leaving the center area empty to use for pinning up pictures, notes, and souvenirs.

PENCIL HOLDERS

Pencil holders can be made in several ways. Find a jar, can, or other container to use as a base. Then cover this base either with burlap or sand. Before you add the covering to the outside, you may wish to spray the inside of the container with flat black paint or cover it with black felt. Even though the inside isn't visible after you get pencils and pens in the holder, the paint or felt will give it a more finished look. To protect your furniture from scratches, glue another piece of felt to the bottom on the outside as well. If the container seems a little unstable, glue lead weights to the bottom before gluing on the felt covering.

Covering the outside of your container with burlap is quite easy. If you painted the inside of the container, make sure the paint is dry. Cut the burlap to fit, leaving enough material to fold over the top edge of the container. The edge will look best if the material is folded under so that no ragged ends show. It will be neater if you first press the folded edge with an iron or tack with thread. Glue the material to the container and let it dry thoroughly.

Covering with sand is slightly more difficult. Get some sand the color you want and a small strainer. With a brush spread glue over one side of the container. Then dust it with sand by gradually sifting sand through a strainer until the side is covered. Let it dry. Continue this process until the whole container is covered evenly with sand. Let the glue dry completely. If you notice any bare spots, dab on more glue and sand. When your last glue application dries, shake off any loose sand and spray the entire piece with clear acrylic to fix it.

After your base is covered either with burlap or sand and the glue is dry, finish the pencil holder by gluing a starfish, sand dollar, or other sea treasure emblem to the front of your pencil holder.

BOOKENDS

Cut weathered boards to make bookends or restyle some old bookends in the same manner as the pencil holders above. Cover bricks or wooden bookends with burlap. If you prefer, stain or antique wooden bookends to look like driftwood. Glue a starfish, shells, or beach glass as a design on the finished surface which will be visible when the book ends are in use.

Claude Bonang, the creator of the starfish people, adds some special touches to the bookends that he makes. He first cuts plywood to fit a standard metal bookend. He then glues or screws the plywood to the metal so that the original metal bookend is kind of like a skeleton. To make the bookend more stable, he glues lead weights to the bottom and then covers the plywood with burlap, gluing it in the center and stapling the edges to the back and bottom of the plywood. He glues felt to the bottom and inside edges of the bookend. Then he cuts lobster traps slats to size, varnishes them, and uses the pieces to frame the bookend side which is exposed. Finally he glues shells, and other items from his collection, to the finished surface. He follows the same procedure for the second bookend of the pair. When these bookends are in use, a framed piece of beach art is visible on either side.

BEACH GLASS OR SHELL NIGHT LIGHTS

Do you have any plain plastic night lights that glow dimly when plugged into a wall outlet? Dress them up by gluing small shells or beach glass to the plastic. It's easy, and so pretty when the light shines through in the dark!

Night light made with epoxy and beach glass to resemble stained glass

Night light created with beach glass. Small translucent shells or pieces of shells could be used instead

I found some inexpensive plastic night lights which were made to look like old-fashioned laterns. Using clear glue made especially for plastic, I covered the white parts of the lantern with different colors of beach glass. It's important to get the glue which is made to use on plastics, because regular craft glue may not hold the beach glass to the plastic night light for long.

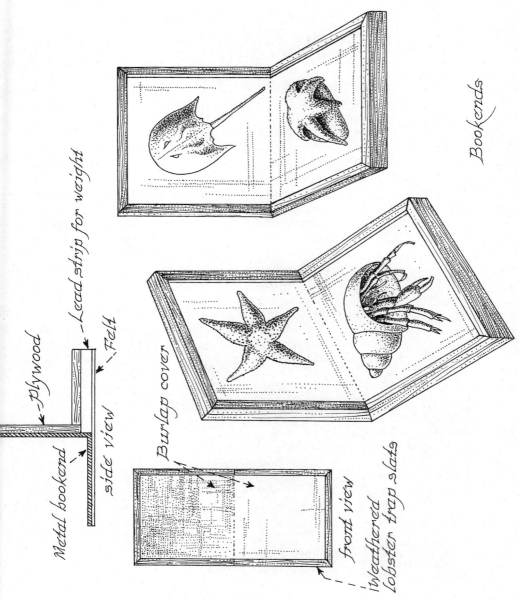

Bookends

Plywood

Lead strip for weight

Felt

side view

Metal bookend

Burlap cover

front view

Weathered Lobster trap slats

113

If you're more ambitious and want a more dramatic effect, use the black/gray epoxy to outline each piece of glass as you attach it to a plain night light. See directions for using the epoxy in Chapter 6, "Using Beach Glass to Resemble Stained Glass."

Both of these beach glass night lights are so beautiful when lighted that they no longer look like cheap night lights purchased at a discount store.

REFRIGERATOR MAGNETS FROM SHELLS, DRIFTWOOD, AND BEACH GLASS

If you like to attach notes and children's school papers to your refrigerator door, you probably use magnets. Magnets of several types are simple and inexpensive to make.

One mail order catalog offers four tiny shell magnets for $2.99! Find your best shells, glue a magnet to the back and they're ready to use for a lot less than $2.99. The best part is that you get to chose your own shells instead of taking what the mail order company would send.

Use driftwood for magnets. Some small, unusually shaped pieces of driftwood will be interesting as they are. Just glue a magnet to the back of each. Most craft shops sell magnet strips which can easily be cut to size.

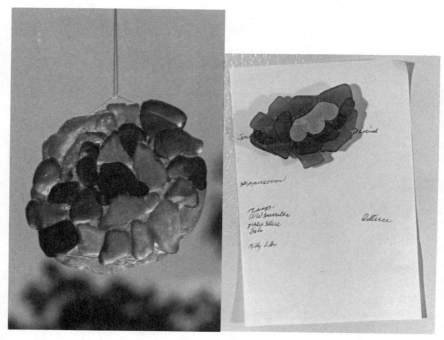

Beach glass suncatcher   Beach glass refrigerator magnet

**Wooden whole cutout covered with tiny periwinkles
can hang on a Christmas tree or decorate a kitchen**

Find or cut a piece of driftwood into a square about 2″ x 2″. Draw or write on the wood with white or black ink or paint. For example, try "I love beachcoming" or a simple sketch of a seal, starfish, or sea gull. Or simply glue tiny shells or bits of beach glass to the wood. Attach a magnet to the back of each.

If it's small, the beach glass suncatcher described below won't look as pretty withut light shining through it, but it can be made into a magnet for your refrigerator or file cabinet.

In Chapter 10 you'll also find directions for making mouse and owl magnets.

BEACH GLASS SUNCATCHER

Beach glass suncatchers hanging in a window will capture the sun's rays and remind you of a sunny summer day on the beach, even in January when snow covers the ground and it's below zero outside.

To make a suncatcher find a piece of beach glass about three inches in diameter for the base. Since one side will be covered with smaller pieces of glass, your base piece needs to be worn well only on one side, the side you **don't** cover. White glass is best for the base so the light will shine through the colors of the smaller pieces when your suncatcher hangs in the window. Choose a number of well-worn, smaller pieces of glass to glue on top of the base in any design you choose. Very small pieces of glass look best in the suncatcher.

Before you glue any glass to the base, try arranging the pieces in various ways on your base. When you are satisfied with the design, glue the small pieces in place. Use only a small amount of glue which will dry clear. Try to keep the glue from squishing out between pieces of glass. Use a cotton swab or toothpick to mop up the excess glue before it dries. When the glue is completely dry, wrap transparent line around the suncatcher's edges and tie securely in a knot. The line will catch between the base and the top pieces of glass. Then add a loop for hanging the finished suncatcher in a window where it will catch the rays of the sun. Craft stores also sell clear plastic suction cups with hooks for hanging items directly on window glass.

These suncatchers can also be ornaments for your Christmas tree. Make them small so they aren't too heavy to hang. If you don't have the right pieces of beach glass to use for suncatcher or ornament bases or want to make lighter weight ones, cut bases from plastic sheeting material or a clear plastic coffee can cover. Punch a hole for hanging on a hook, and, leaving this hole clear, glue small pieces of colored glass to cover the surface. Be sure to use glue made especially for plastic or the glass won't adhere to the plastic for long.

You can also play around with the beach glass pieces in your collection to see if you can make a recognizable design on the ornament. For example, I found by gluing three pieces of glass on a clear plastic circle, I could make a fairly accurate representation of a sailboat under full sail. Two triangular pieces formed the mainsail and jib. A thinner piece, slightly wider at one end than the other became the hull. It's fun to fool around with beach glass. You never know what you might come up with!

BEACH GLASS PAPERWEIGHT

You can use the same method to make the beach glass paperweight, except that you should choose a larger and somewhat heavier piece of glass for the base piece. Any shape will do, but the base piece should be about 3" x 3" or larger. Since you need more weight for the paperweight, you can glue smaller pieces of glass on top in layers. Be sure one layer dries before you add another one. Again, play around with the placement of your smaller pieces before you actually glue them.

You can define the pieces of glass with sand if you wish. Put glue between the pieces of glass as well as under them. While the glue is still wet, use a small strainer to sift sand over the paperweight. When the glue is dry, shake off the excess sand. If you have a big enough base piece, you can also make a candleholder in this manner. See Chapter 6, "Sand Candles."

JEWELRY, DESK, OR PILL BOX WITH BEACH GLASS OR SHELLS

Would you like a small beach glass box to hold costume jewelry on your dresser, or paper clips and rubber bands on your desk? Any clear plastic or glass box can be used as the base. Glue small pieces of beach

Beach glass paperweight

glass to the four sides and cover. Follow the same procedure using shells instead of beach glass if you'd like one made of shells. A small wooden box would be okay to cover with shells since you can't see through them the way you can through the glass.

Consider renovating an old jewelry box you already have by covering it with shells or glass, or look around for containers for products which could be transformed. For example, some dried fruits come in little plastic boxes which are the perfect size for jewelry boxes. You should find everything you need right around the house if you keep your eyes open!

If you have found an especially beautiful or rare shell, make it a gift for a friend by putting it in a shell or beach glass box. Your friend can display the shell on a bookcase shelf and use the box on a vanity or desk.

SHELL OR BEACH GLASS VASE

Cover a nondescript vase, or one of the jars that comes with a well-known brand of packaged salad dressing mix, with shells or beach glass. You can use the black and gray epoxy to give the vase the look of stained glass. See the directions for making the candleholder in Chapter 6. Or you can just use clear glue to attach the beach glass or shells. Fill the vase with dried flowers or the cat-o-nine tails you cut at the roadside on your way home from the beach.

SEA URCHIN DESIGNS

Jon Ross makes two very interesting arrangements with sea urchins. For a small vase holding dried flowers, he glues a sea urchin shell upside down to a small piece of driftwood. Then he fills the urchin vase with a tiny bouquet of dried flowers, gluing the flowers in to make them stay put.

A sea urchin becomes a mushroom in another of his arrangements. The sea urchin shell turned upside down is glued to a stalk, really a small piece of driftwood. The stalk is then glued to a scallop shell base or a driftwood base. Jon surrounds the mushroom with pieces of beach glass, bits of seaweed, pretty pebbles, or other shells, all artistically arranged and then glued to the base.

SHELL PICKS FOR HORS D'OUEVRES

Would you like something special for a summer party? Collect and clean some tiny snail or periwinkle shells. Glue one to one end of each cocktail toothpick. Fill a tiny glass with these shell picks when you put out the hors d'ouevres for your guests. A shot glass is the right size.

NAPKIN RINGS

Glue small shells or pieces of beach glass to a ring of wood or cloth to hold napkins when you serve a special summer meal.

PLACE CARD HOLDERS

Glue a couple of shells or pieces of beach glass together, leaving a crevice on the top without glue, to hold a card with the guest's name. Or decorate cork floats with sea glass and shells and cut a small slit to hold the card. If you're short of cork floats, cut them into smaller pieces and make two or three card holders from each float.

GIFT TAGS AND GREETING CARDS

Dress up plain gift tags or greeting cards by gluing real shells or sand dollars to them as decorations. Better yet, make your own tags or cards using stiff or parchment-finished paper. In addition to shells, consider using bits of seaweed along with the shells to create your own design. Red seaweed looks very dramatic on ivory paper! Even if your not clever with words, your visual greeting along with a simple "Happy Birthday" will be something unique and special.

SHELL CASTLES

Give the kids a new project to keep them busy on a rainy afternoon. With glue and plenty of shells, they can build their own castles by gluing shells to each other. Or if they prefer, they can cut castles or houses from cardboard, tape them together, and then finish by gluing on shells to cover the cardboard frame.

SEA SHADOW BOX

These shadow boxes are both attractive and easy to make. Buy an acrylic frame 4 x 6 inches, 1 ¼ inches deep, available in most discount, department, and drug stores where picture frames are sold. The frame will stand on its side for placement on a shelf, but the cardboard backing also has a pull-out stand and a tab for hanging on the wall.

Take the cardboard insert out and cover with a thin material for your backing: burlap, other cloth, paper, or coat with glue and sand. You may need more than one coat of sand to cover in some spots if you don't make sure you have glue covering the whole surface the first time. When the glue is dry, shake off any loose sand. Spray the sand with clear acrylic to fix it. Plan your arrangement of seaweed, beach glass, or small, thin shells, or whatever you want to include. When you're satisfied with your design, glue the items to the backing. Insert the cardboard back into the frame.

Although the cardboard insert doesn't need to fit as snugly when you're finished as it did before you started, you'll have to limit what you include in this shadow box to sea treasures which measure a quarter of an inch or less in depth.

If you want to use larger items, make (or have someone make for you) a wooden box with glass on the top, bottom, and two sides, leaving one of

Sea urchin mushroom by Jon Ross   Shell picks for hors d'ouevres

Half of cork float, and beach glass place card holders

the two remaining wood sides unattached. Stain, antique, or varnish the wood as desired. When it is dry, stand the box with one wooden side down and load sand, shells, or whatever else you want in your three-dimensional shadow box. Some items can be glued to each other. Others can be anchored in sand. When you're finished arranging the treasures inside, put the top on and nail it down.

Sea shadow box made with shells and seaweed

TILE PLAQUE WITH BEACH GLASS OR SHELLS

The tile plaque is another project easy enough for children to make by themselves. Buy a ceramic tile. Attach picture wire or other means of hanging to the back with epoxy. Then create a design for the front using beach glass or shells. Move the pieces around until you have the design that pleases you. Then glue each piece to the tile. When the glue is dry, the plaque is ready to hang on the wall.

MIRRORS AND PICTURE FRAMES DRESSED UP IN SEA GLASS OR SHELLS

Rejuvenate an old picture frame or mirror by gluing a border of shells or sea glass all around its sides. If your frame is a fairly flat one of wood, consider defining each shell or piece of glass with sand. As you glue each shell on, spread glue around the shell as well and sift sand over the top. When the glue is dry, shake off the excess sand and spray with clear acrylic to fix it.

BEACH SCULPTURE

Make your own abstract sculpture by combining driftwood, rocks, and shells or beach glass in a free-standing artwork. If your bottom piece of

Beach glass sailboat mounted on plastic. Hang in window or on Christmas tree

Beach glass flower design mounted on tile

121

driftwood isn't stable enough by itself, nail or glue it with epoxy to a weathered, stained, antiqued, or sand-covered plywood board base.

SEAWEED PAINTING

Arrange wet seaweed of different colors in a design on a piece of fairly stiff paper. Put another sheet of paper on top to absorb extra water. Cover with a heavy book and let dry. Most of the time the seaweed will be stuck to the paper, but if not, glue loose pieces in place. When the glue dries, mat and frame your painting, or mount it on a flat piece of driftwood.

SEA GLASS "PAINTING"

This "painting" is actually a collage. Get a clear pane of glass the size you want your finished piece to be. Lay out the beach glass to form the design or scene you want to create. Then attach beach glass to the clear glass with glue which dries clear.

Your finished "painting" will look best if you stand it in a window through which the sun shines. You may want to try this project using epoxy so the finished piece looks like a stained glass window. See the directions for using the black and gray epoxy that were given for the candleholder resembling stained glass in Chapter 6.

CRAFT SHOP SHOPPING

There really is no end to the ideas you can come up with for using your beachcoming treasures. In walking around a craft shop recently, I came up with the following ideas for combining the results of my beach- combing with products sold for other purposes in the craft shop.

The little bird's nests and wooden baskets could be filled with shells, tied with a small bow, and used as party favors or place cards holders. They have wooden cutouts of ducks, teddy bears, cats, and others, which are intended for tole painting. Instead you could cover them with sea glass or shells, and hang them in a window or on a Christmas tree. I used a little wooden whale cutout for a Christmas wreath decoration this year. I covered the surface of the cutout by gluing tiny periwinkle shells all over it. Then I used a black felt tip marker to color one of the periwinkle shells black so the tiny whale had an eye.

Plastic needlecraft matting or copper sheeting could be cut and used as a base for beach glass or shell Christmas tree ornaments. The hair comb, which I suppose was meant to be dressed up with beads or sequins, could be decorated with small pieces of beach glass, tiny shells, or shell chips. Straw baskets can be made into beachcombing specials when they're adorned on top with a few shells or pieces of beach glass.

Walk around your local craft shop or the crafts and notions section of a department store. What could you do with the items displayed? You'll be surprised how creative you can be, once you start looking for new ways to use your beachcombing finds. And if you come up with a new combination, you can be sure that what you make is truly one-of-a-kind!

SHELL OR SEA GLASS MOSAIC OR TRIVET

One material you can use for this project is plaster of paris. Find a mold the size you want the finished plaque or trivet to be. Foil pans, either rand or square, will work well. If your mold is more than 4 inches in diameter, you should also cut a piece of screen or wire mesh to fit the mold so that the finished product will have additional strength. Grease the mold lightly with cooking or mineral oil.

Cut a piece of newspaper the same size as your mold and use it to plan the arrangement of shells and beach glass. When you've got the design you want, mix the plaster. The mixture should be stiff enough to spread in the mold, not runny. Fill the mold. If you're using a screen, put some plaster in. Spread. Add screen and cover with the rest of the plaster. Then, move the shells or glass you have laid out on the newspaper, to the corresponding places on the plaster in the mold.

When the plaster is dry, remove it from the mold and spray it with clear acrylic or glaze to protect the surface from moisture. Glue a piece of felt to the back and a hook if you want to hang your mosaic on the wall. Another option is mounting the mosaic to a driftwood backing before hanging. Without a hook, the mosaic can be used on the table as a trivet.

Polyester casting resin (standard inventory in most craft shops) can also be used to make mosaic tiles which can be used as wall decorations, trivets, or to form a new top for a table. See Chapter 5. Get molds the size and shape you want. Square pliable plastic food containers make good molds.

Cut newspaper the same size and shape as your mold. Arrange shells or sea glass on the newspaper. When your design is set, fill the mold with resin. Add catalyst and stir to mix. Then put shells or glass into resin-filled mold to match the design you have laid out on the newsprint. Let dry. Remove from mold. Glue on a felt backing or a hook for hanging, if desired.

Driftwood can also be used as a base for the resin mosaic. Instead of a mold, hollow out a flat piece of driftwood. Decide how you want to arrange your shells or glass. Fill the hollowed-out space with resin, following the same procedure outlined above.

SAND PAINTING

Sand painting is a good activity to suggest to children who say, "There's nothing to do." Collect sand of different colors or mix sand with powdered paint. Draw a design on a piece of paper with glue and sprinkle with sand. After the glue dries, shake off the excess sand.

Another way to do a sand painting is to draw a simple picture lightly in pencil on a piece of paper. Label each part with the color you want to paint it, kind of a do-it-yourself paint-by-the-number project. Begin with one color of sand first. Spread glue on all areas of the picture that require that color. Sprinkle with sand. Let dry. Shake off the excess sand, and repeat the process with the rest of the colors, one at a time.

CRUSHED SHELLS PAINTING

Follow the same procedures described above except that you "paint" with finely crushed shells mixed with powdered paint instead of sand. The finished painting will have a little more depth than a sand painting.

Even a misshapen evergreen wreath looks better with shells and sea treasures. Starfish on the bow were painted to look like Santa Clauses

CHAPTER 12

BRING THE SEASIDE HOME FOR THE HOLIDAYS OR ANYTIME

If you're like many people, you love the holidays in winter as well as summers at the seashore. Combine both by using your beachcombing treasures gathered during the summer to decorate your house for the holidays. And then make that summer vacation seem to last all year long by fixing up a porch or patio to look like a summer seaside retreat which you can enjoy even when the snow is deep!

The seashore also provides many good things to eat. When you're picking up shells, driftwood, and sea glass to use for crafts you plan to make later, also bring home some "beachcombed" edibles for your gastronomic pleasure right now.

CHRISTMAS FROM THE SEA

Centerpiece and Candles

That driftwood centerpiece that you made for your dining table (Chapter 11 "Simple Driftwood Designs") can be dressed up for Christmas with red candles and evergreen boughs. Add a reindeer or Santa figure if your centerpiece isn't too busy. You can easily make another to grace a buffet or hall table. Red votive candles can be set in quahog shells and placed around the house. And if you made the candleholders which resemble stained glass (Chapter 6), they'll look festive set in among some evergreen boughs. They'll also smell more like Christmas if you burn bayberry- or pine-scented candles in them.

Wreath Ideas

Would you like a Christmas wreath for your door which doesn't look just like your neighbor's? Make your own evergreen wreath or buy one undecorated except for the obligatory red bow. Then tie shells, starfish, or sand dollars to the wreath before you hang it.

I made my Christmas wreath several years ago and can still use it because I useed vines as a base rather than evergreens. Make your own vine wreath from ivy or grape vines or buy one ready-made from a craft shop. I tied some of the shells to the wreath with thin wire; others were just tucked in between the vines. A big white velveteen bow and an artificial poinsettia give the wreath its Christmas spirit. Just by changing the color of the bow and the flower, I can use it to say "Happy Easter" or "Happy Thanksgiving."

If you prefer, you can decorate a pine cone wreath with shells. To make a small pine cone and shell wreath, cut a circle from cardboard, 3 to 4 inches in diameter. Glue pine cones and shells to the base, selecting a larger shell or starfish to replace the traditional bow. Finish by gluing a piece of felt to the back.

For a larger wreath you'll need a tiered wire wreath as a base. Glue large pine cones or tie them with thin wire to cover the wreath base. Then glue shells, either a variety or all the same kind, to the pine cones. Small starfish can be glued in among the shells. Consider a large starfish (5″ or more) instead of a bow.

You can also make a wreath entirely from shells and other sea treasures. Cut a circle out of cardboard the size you want your finished wreath to be. Use it as the base on which to glue shells. Decorate the finished wreath with sprigs of holly and tiny red and green bows.

Ornaments

Ornaments for your Christmas tree can come right from the beach as well. What about a starfish wired to the very tip of your tree? Drill tiny holes in shells and sand dollars and use transparent line to hang them on the tree. Starfish and beach glass can be hung by first tying the line around them and then making a loop for hanging. To secure the line, glue it directly to the starfish or beach glass. For more color use curling ribbon to tie little green, red, and gold bows to the tips of starfish arms.

If they're not too heavy, very small beach glass suncatchers make wonderful Christmas ornaments. See the directions for making these in Chapter 11, "Beach Glass Suncatcher." The owl and mouse magnets as well as some of the other animals described in Chapter 10 can also be

Wreath made from grape vines decorated with shells and other sea treasures, an artificial pointsettia, and velvet bow

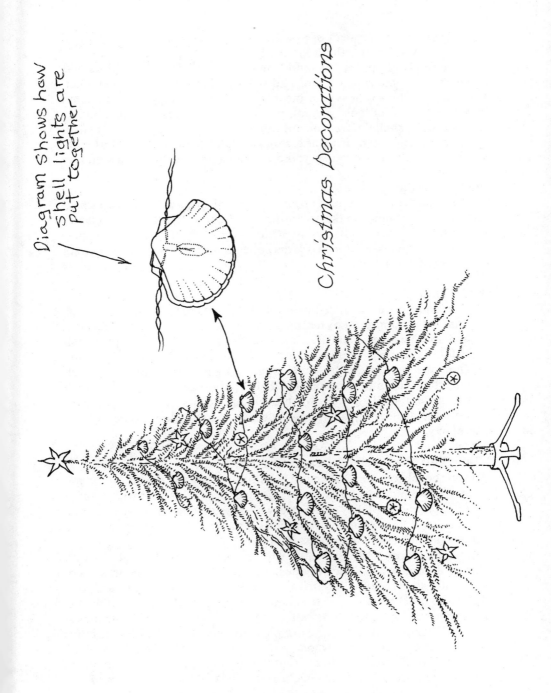

Diagram shows how shell lights are put together

Christmas Decorations

used as ornaments. Instead of attaching a magnet backing, tie a loop of transparent line around them for hanging.

If you're more ambitious and somewhat artistic, paint Christmas scenes inside some shells. Clam and scallop shells will work best. Quahog shells will be too heavy for most trees. If you aren't concerned about preserving a natural look, you can paint starfish to look like little Santas You can make shells more colorful by gluing red, green, gold, and silver sparkles to them. Then string and hang. Drill holes in all the shells before you begin decorating them so you don't mess up the work you've done.

Shell Garlands

As a replacement for mass-produced tinsel garland or an old-fashioned popcorn chain, make your own shell chain. Drill small holes in periwinkle and snail shells and then string them together using transparent thread or line. You'll need a large collection of shells to make a chain of any length.

Shell Lights

One man in my area made beautiful shell lights for his Christmas tree. He gathered a number of oyster and scallop shells from local fishermen, cleaned and bleached them. Then he glued two shells together over each tiny white light on a regular string of Christmas tree lights. The only problem, of course, is the the shells must be unglued to replace a burned-out bulb, but the simple and beautiful effect of the lights shining through the translucent shells is well worth overcoming this difficulty. To facilitate bulb replacement in shell lights, be sure to use a glue less permanent than epoxy.

A Tiny Tree This Year—A Grand One Next Year

If your beachcombing collection isn't large enough at this point for you to make enough decorations for a large tree, begin this year with a small tree on a table completely decorated with seaside treasures. Next Christmas you'll will have enough decorations for a large tree if you plan ahead and beachcomb more often next summer.

However, there's nothing wrong with mixing seaborn decorations with more traditional ones. One very beautiful tree I saw this year was decorated with shells, sand dollars, and starfish along with tiny sailboat, whale, and other purchased ornaments in keeping with a nautical theme. As I mentioned in Chapter 11, you can purchase wooden cutouts meant for tole painting—a whale, for example—and glue on tiny shells or chips of beach glass to cover the wood.

Creating your own Christmas from the sea will give you the perfect excuse for spending more time beachcombing. What better way could you spend those wonderful summer days?

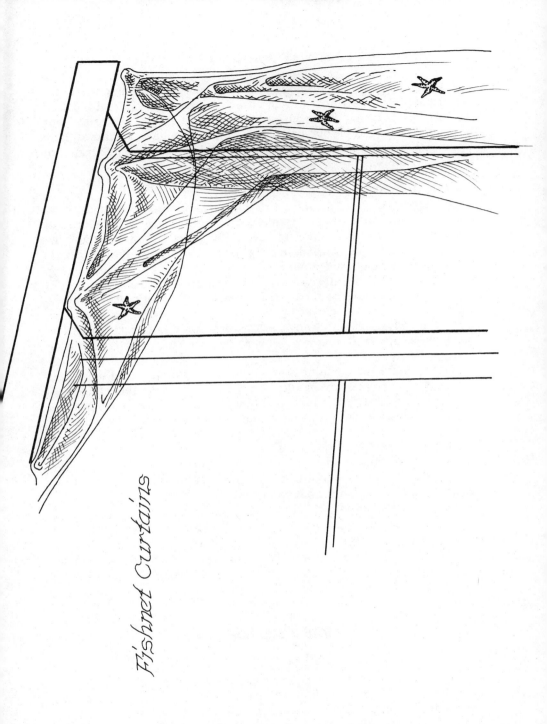

Fishnet Curtains

YEAR-ROUND VACATIONING AT HOME

But even when there's no holiday to celebrate and summer vacation's months away, you can create a very attractive seaside escape right in your own home. Not only will you have the perfect place to display your beachcrafts and store your collection, you'll also have an atmosphere which encourages you to relax because you'll have created the illusion of being near the sea.

Seaside Retreat

Do you have a study, or a patio room or a sunporch that you'd like to transform into your at-home home by the shore? Drape fishnet around windows instead of curtains. Use cork floats to gather and tie the "curtain" ends. Hook small starfish into the fishnet in various places for decoration. Hang a sea-based mobile or shell wind chime from the ceiling. Place large pieces of driftwood for room accents or in the plants. Add a lobster trap table and quahog shell ashtrays. Don't forget to include a driftwood lamp. Hang lobster buoys from the ceiling and on the walls.

Fill glass decanters or brandy snifters with shells and beach glass. The beach glass should sit near a window so you can enjoy the light shining through the colored glass. If you sort your beach glass by size and/or color before you fill the containers, you'll be able to quickly find the pieces you need when you're working on a craft. Meanwhile the collection is attractively displayed rather than taking up needed closet space. Make a driftwood sign of welcome or with the family name to hang over the door.

Landscaping and Storage Ideas

Outside use rocks, shells, and driftwood as accents in your landscaping. If you're industrious and like gardening, use your rock collection to make a rock garden. Collect flat rocks to make garden paths through your flowers or a walkway to your door. Many pathways in the Bahamas are lined with large conch shells. Use your extra shells and beach glass for ground cover around plants. They look good and will weather more as well. You'll know where they are when you need some for crafts. Smaller pieces of driftwood can be stored outside in the same way, or you can weather your own wood for specific projects.

INCREDIBLE EDIBLES

Finding good things to eat at the seashore doesn't mean that you have to sit for hours on a wharf or large rock, fishing pole in hand, waiting for the fish to bite. Many incredible edibles can be gathered (**mussels** or **sea veggies**, for example), dug (**clams**), or purchased (**lobster**). In this section you'll read about only some of the many gastronomical delights you can find by the sea. Because of differences in geography and climate, you'll

Chondrus
(Irish Moss)

Ulva
(Sea Lettuce)

131

find different varieties of sea plants and animals in different regions. Find out what plants and animals are native to your favorite seacoast area.

Sea Veggies

Edible kelp, or alaria, can be found on both the Pacific and Atlantic coasts. Alaria, brown or olive brown in color, grows up to 12" attached to rocks and ledges. You can recognize alaria by its long, ruffled fronds; it will be exposed at low tide. When you cut the sinuous fronds to bring home, leave at least 3" attached to the rocks so the plant will continue to grow.

Wash the kelp in salt water. Then dry it in the sun or a warm oven (100 to 150 degrees), leaving the oven door open an inch or two so that moisture can escape. Alaria can be stored in airtight containers or plastic bags. Before using dried alaria, cover it with fresh water and soak overnight.

Alaria can be added to salad greens, used as a flavoring in soups and stews, or mixed with other vegetables in a stir-fry recipe.

Sea lettuce, or ulva, is bright yellowish-green in color, grows from 1 inch to 1 foot long on the Atlantic, Gulf, and Pacific coasts. It's found in exposed areas near the low tide mark on rocks and in tide pools. It thrives in brackish water where there is decaying organic matter. Its wide, slightly curled leaves look somewhat like limp garden-grown leaf lettuce.

Wash sea lettuce in fresh water and shred into fine strips—it's very chewy. Mix it in with garden salads to add color and a different texture, or use it in soups.

A West Coast sea veggie, **green nori,** can be found alone or in groups of plants growing near the high tide mark. Usually unbranched, nori plants range from ½ inch to one foot. Peak harvest time is early spring. **Red nori,** actually ranging in color from steel-gray to purple-brown, grows on rocks at the mid-tide mark. It can be gathered in the late spring when its deeply ruffled fronds are 3 to 5 inches long or later when the fronds have grown to 2 or 3 feet.

Nori fronds can be dried (like alaria above) and crumbled into flakes to be sprinkled over eggs or egg dishes, salads, soups, or casseroles. Nori also makes an interesting hors d'ouevre. Wash the fronds in cold water. Shake off excess water and then pat dry between two sheets of paper towel. Tear nori into 5" pieces and spread out on screen or wire baking racks. Nori needs maximum air exposure. Then bake in 200 degree oven with the door open slightly (1 to 2 inches to allow moisture to escape) for 30 minutes, turning fronds over when their edges are dry (about 15 minutes). When the nori is very crisp, it's ready to eat right away sprinkled with salt and dipped in peanut oil or your favorite chip dip.

Irish moss, a sea vegetable which grows on both sides of the North Atlantic, can be found exposed at low tide on rocky shores in loose clumps. Irish moss has a tightly curled leaf or blade, is usually 2 to 4 inches long, and its color ranges from a deep red to sometimes almost purple. Swish and soak Irish moss in several changes of fresh water and then dry it as you would alaria. Crumble fresh or dried Irish moss into small pieces to flavor and thicken soups and stews.

Irish moss can also be used to make an unusual pudding. Here is the recipe.

Irish Moss Pudding

½ cup Irish moss
2 cups milk
½ tsp. salt
½ cup honey
1½ cups fresh strawberies (or other fruit)
8″ square piece of cheesecloth

Gather at least a half-cup of Irish moss. Cover it with fresh, cold water and soak for 30 minutes, changing the water several times. Drain. Then tie up the Irish moss into a bag made from a piece of cheesecloth about 8″ square.

Heat 2 cups of milk in a double-boiler. Suspend the cheesecloth bag in the milk and simmer. Stir constantly, pressing the bag against the side of the pan every once in a while to release the Irish moss gel. When the mixture thickens (about 20–30 minutes), remove from heat. Throw Irish moss away.

Puree 1½ cups fresh strawberries, or other fruit, with ½ cup honey in a blender. Add milk mixture and ½ tsp. salt. Blend at high speed. Pour pudding into covered container and refrigerate for 2 hours. Serve garnished with whipped cream and sliced strawberries, if desired.

If you'd like to know more about sea vegetables, the bibliography lists some sources. If you live in the San Francisco Bay area, you might want to get in touch with Alice Green. She conducts workshops to show other people how to find and prepare sea vegetables to eat and has compiled an illustrated "Gathering Guide" and recipes for fresh and packaged sea vegetables. To get further information on her guide or upcoming workshops write to her at 1326 A Sixth Avenue, San Francisco, CA 94122 or call her at (415) 633-1200.

Periwinkles

Edible periwinkles can be found along the Atlantic Coast to the Gulf of Mexico. Periwinkles are usually no larger than an inch around. The "northern" variety is usually gray in color with brown or red bands while it's "southern" cousin is normally yellow with brown spots.

When you gather periwinkles to eat, collect only those that are stuck to seaweed, rocks, or pilings. That way you'll be sure they're alive.

Boil or steam the periwinkles until the operculum ("little door") opens. Throw this lid away. Pick the meat out with a safety pin or needle. They are curled into their shells and can be twisted out. Save the shells to use in your craft projects.

The periwinkles are ready to eat as they are now, dipped in melted butter, or drain them on paper towels and try one of the recipes below.

Baked Periwinkles

6 dozen periwinkles (Cook first and clean meat from shells)
½ cup butter (at room temperature)
¼ cup dried parsley
1 T. finely chopped scallions
2 cloves garlic (minced)
24 large clam, quahog, or snail shells (or 4 small glass baking cups)

Cream all ingredients except periwinkle meat and shells. Mix periwinkle meat with butter mixture. Let stand for 2 hours and then stuff into shells or baking cups. Set shells or baking cups on cookie sheet. Bake in 450 degree oven until browned (about 10 minutes). Serve in shells or cups to be spread on warm slices of French bread or crackers. Serves 4.

Marinated Winkles

Steam periwinkles and clean meat from shells. Put the periwinkles in a glass jar with a tightly-fitting cover. Cover with oil and vinegar. Add a few onion slices and fresh, slivered garlic. Add a dash of pepper and a pinch of oregano. Shake well and refrigerate for 24 hours, shaking periodically during this time. Eat individually with your fingers or toothpicks or serve on crackers.

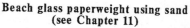
Beach glass paperweight using sand
(see Chapter 11)

Other Recipes for Clams and Mussels

See Chapter 2 for directions on digging clams and gathering mussels.

Clam, Mussel, or Periwinkle Spaghetti Sauce

Make your favorite spaghetti sauce. Then, instead of meatballs or ground beef, use meat which has been cooked and cleaned from clams, mussels, or periwinkles. Serve on pasta.

My Father's Castine Clam Chowder

1 quart fresh clams
4 cups diced potatoes
1 onion (chopped)
1 small piece of salt pork or 1 slice uncooked bacon
1 can evaporated milk OR 1 cup half-and-half
1 quart regular milk
1 T. butter
salt and pepper to taste

Steam the cleaned clams in a small amount of sea water in a large pot. Salted water will do if you don't have sea water. The clams are done when they open (about 5–10 minutes). Save the water from the clams.

Let clams cool and then remove from shells. "Heads," the black tips of soft shell clams, may be cut off and discarded, although they are good to eat. Cut large clams in half.

Peal and dice potatoes and chop up onion. Put potatoes, onion, and salt pork or bacon in water saved from clams. Use only enough liquid to cover ingredients. Boil until potatoes are done—firm, not mushy. Add clams, evaporated milk or half-and-half to potato mixture. Slow heat to blend all ingredients. This mixture is the chowder base and may be refrigerated until ready for use.

When ready to serve chowder, add 1 quart milk (or less, if desired), butter and seasoning to taste, to chowder base. Heat slowly so as not to curdle, milk. Full recipe will serve 6–8 people.

If you wish, make smaller amounts of chowder from the base by adding less regular milk. Remaining base may be saved and made up later.

Fried Clams in Batter

32 soft- or hard-shell clams (shucked and cleaned)
1 egg (separated)
½ cup milk
1 T. melted butter
¼ tsp. salt
½ cup sifted flour

Beat the egg yolk together with half of the milk and the melted butter. Add salt to flour. Sift together and add to egg mixture. Beat until smooth. Stir in remaining milk. Beat egg white stiff and fold into mixture.

Dip each clam into the batter and fry in deep fat or oil (about 375 degrees) until golden brown, turning frequently. Drain on paper towel. Serves 4.

Fried Clams in Crumbs

32 soft- or hard-shell clams (shucked and cleaned)
¼ to ½ cup flour
½ to 1 cup milk
1 cup cornflake or cracker crumbs

Dip each clam in flour, then in milk, and finally in crumbs. Fry in deep fat or oil (375 degrees) until golden brown on all sides. Drain on paper towel. Serves 4.

Broiled Cherrystone Clams (or Northern Quahogs) on the Half-Shell

2 dozen cherrystones on the half-shell
3–4 slices bacon, chopped but uncooked
3 T. minced onion
3 T. minced green pepper
1T. dried parsley
2 T. lemon juice

Fry bacon until partly cooked. Add onion, pepper, and parsley and cook until soft but not browned. Put clams on broiler pan. Sprinkle with lemon juice. Top with bacon mixture, spreading evenly among clams. Broil until hot (about 4–5 minutes). Serves 4–5 people.

Baked Cherrystones (or Northern Quahogs) on the Half-Shell

2 dozen cherrystones on the half-shell
3 cloves garlic (minced)
2 T. dried parsley
1 tsp. oregano
½ cup fresh bread crumbs
¼ grated Parmesan cheese
1 .T melted butter
lemon wedges

Put clams in shallow baking pan. Mix garlic, parsley, oregano, bread crumbs, and cheese together. Add melted butter to moisten. Distribute the mixture evenly among clams. Bake in 400 degree oven for 8–10 minutes. Serve with lemon wedges. Serves 4–5.

Kate's Mussels in Wine Sauce

6 quarts fresh mussels
2 cups light, dry white wine
½ cup minced onion (or green onion)
6 T. butter
½ bay leaf
¼ tsp. thyme
⅛ tsp. pepper
6-8 sprigs parsley

Scrub mussels with stiff brush and cut off beards. Wash thoroughly and soak in bucket of sea water, spreading a thin layer of corn meal on top. (At least two hours, but mussels may soak longer.) Wash mussels again before adding them to wine sauce.

Bring wine and other ingredients except mussels to boil in a large pot (8-10 quart with cover). Boil 2-3 minutes. Add mussels. Cover tightly, and boil quickly over high heat. Shake contents a couple times during cooking so mussels will shift places and cook evenly. Mussels are done when shells open (about 5-10 minutes).

To serve, put mussels on individual dinner plates, pouring liquid over them. Garnish with chopped parsley, if desired. Each person removes mussels from shells with a fork or fingers before eating. Provide a dish for discarded shells. Recipe serves 6-8 people.

Sea Urchins

Part of the spiny green sea urchin is also good to eat. In fact, in Japan sea urchin roe, actually the sea urchin's reproductive organs, is considered to be a delicacy on the same level with caviar.

You can collect living sea urchins from the rocks or ledges at low tide. To get the jelly-like roe out, put the sea urchin on a flat surface (spiny side down) and crack the flat part of the shell open with a hammer. Use a spoon to loosen the gold to orange-colored roe from the five-pointed egg sac. Then lift it out of the shell.

The roe can be eaten as is, spread on crackers. If you wish, sprinkle with lemon juice or Worcestershire sauce. Or you can leave the roe in the shell and use it as a dip for pieces of crusty bread or bread sticks.

If you're camping, you can cook the sea urchins in their shells on the coals of your campfire. Leave them on the fire until their spines burn. Remove. Let them cool until you can touch them without getting burned. Break the warm shells open, remove the roe, and spread it on crackers or French bread.

Here's another recipe to try. If you are unable to collect your own sea urchins, you may be able to find them for sale in a seafood market.

Sea Urchin Pasta

24–30 fresh sea urchins
2 T. olive oil or butter
2 T. finely chopped scallions or chives
dash pepper
1 lb. pasta (any style)
3 T. parsley (chopped or dried)

Crack sea urchins open. Remove the roe and liquid. While the pasta is cooking (almost but not quite to the al dente stage), saute scallions and pepper in olive oil or butter. Add sea urchin roe and liquid. Heat through. Drain pasta but leave it in the pot (or return it to the pot if you drain it in a colander). Strain sea urchin liquid over pasta. Simmer one minute so that pasta will absorb the liquid and cook to al dente. Serve pasta sprinkled with the sea urchin roe mixture which was left in strainer, and top with parsley. Serves 4.

Maine Lobster: The Real Thing!

Fill a container (large enough to contain all the lobters you plan to cook) with water. Bring to a boil. Drop in live lobsters and boil rapidly about 20 minutes for 1 to 1¼ pound lobsters (longer for larger ones). They're ready to serve when the lobster's "feeler" will pull out easily. Give each person one lobster along with nutcracker, pick (to remove meat from shell), and a dish of melted butter in which to dip the lobster meat before eating.

Don't throw away the lobster carcasses after dinner! Save them to make lobster people. Directions can be found in Chapter 10.

HAPPY BEACHCOMBING AND BEACHCRAFTING!

As you continue beachcombing and working with what you collect to create useful and beautiful objects, you'll discover more ways to use what you've found. If you really get hooked on beachcrafting, you'll want to spend more time beachcombing. Go for it! It's great exercise. How else could you enjoy an afternoon so pleasantly, naturally, and inexpensively? You're actually making money as you beachcomb if you use what you get to make gifts instead of buying them. What's more, you can relive the sunny summer hours you spent beachcombing on the dark, cold winter nights when you work on your crafts.

Just think: thousands and thousands of miles of seacoast wait for you. Thousands and thousands of shells and pieces of beach glass await your discovery. Enjoy! Explore!

BIBLIOGRAPHY

FOR FURTHER INFORMATION ON SEA ANIMALS, SHELLS, SEAFOOD, AND SHELLCRAFTS

Abbott, R. Tucker. *How To Know the American Marine Shells*. New York: New American Library, 1970.

Abbott, R. Tucker. *Seashells of the World*. New York: Golden Press, 1985.

Banister, Keith and Campbell, Andrew, editors. *The Encyclopedia of Aquatic Life*. New York: Facts on File, 1985.

Bergeron, Eugene. *How To Clean Seashells*. St. Petersburg: Great Outdoors, 1971.

Boehmer, Raquel. *A Foraging Vacation: Edibles from Maine's Sea and Shore*. Camden, Maine: Down East Books, 1982.

Dance, S. Peter. *The World's Shells*. New York: McGraw-Hill, 1976.

Feinberg, Harold S. *Simon and Schuster's Guide to Shells*. New York: Simon and Schuster, 1980.

Gosner, Kenneth L. *A Field Guide to the Atlantic Seashore*. Boston: Houghton Mifflin, 1978.

Harris, Cricket. *Dictionary of Seashore Life*. St. Petersburg: Great Outdoors, 1961.

Headstrom, Richard. *Lobsters, Crabs, Shrimps and Their Relatives*. New York: A.S. Barnes, 1979.

Kellum, Alice. *Shellcraft Critters*. St. Petersburg: Great Outdoors, 1977.

Lindner, Gert. *Field Guide to Seashells of the World*. New York: Van Nostrand Reinhold, 1978.

Pelosi, Frank and Marjorie. *The Book of Shellcraft Instruction*. St. Petersburg: Great Outdoors, 1959.

Pope, Patricia. *Shellcraft Animals*. St. Petersburg: Great Outdoors, 1975.

Rehder, Harold, ed. *Audubon Society Field Guide to North America*. New York: Knopf, 1981.

Seikman, Lula. *The Great Outdoors Book of Shells*. St. Petersburg: Great Outdoors, 1965.

Seikman, Lula. *Handbook of Shells*. St Petersburg: Great Outdoors, 1981.

Sexton, Gloria V. *Shellcraft Creations*. St. Petersburg: Great Outdoors, 1981.

Sexton, Gloria V. *Shellcraft Necklaces*. St. Petersburg: Great Outdoors, 1981.

Zim, Herbert S. and Ingle, Lester. *Seashores*. New York: Golden Press, 1955.

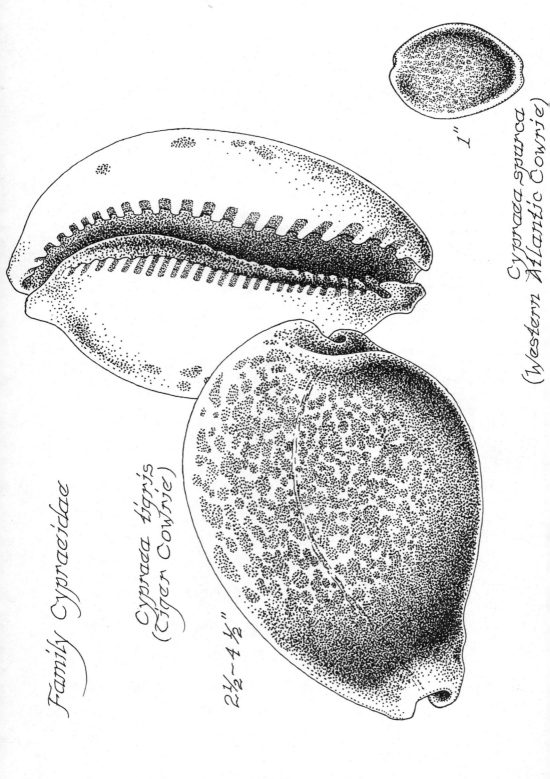

Family Cypraeidae

Cypraea tigris
(Tiger Cowrie)

2½~4½"

Cypraea spurca
Atlantic Cowrie

(Western Atlantic Cowrie)

1"

140

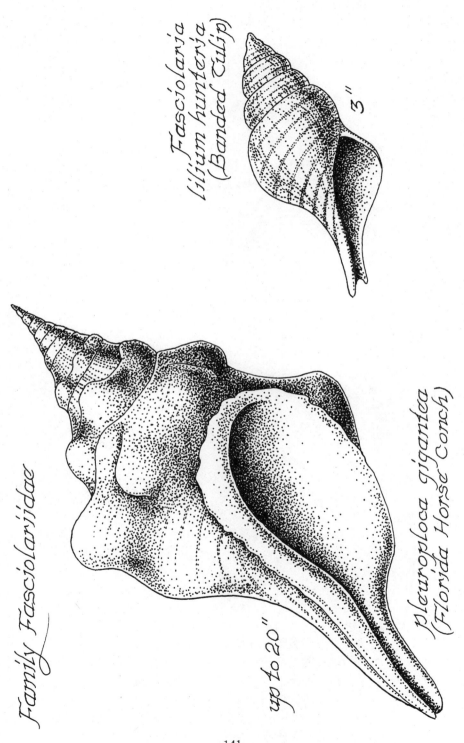

Fasciolaria
lilium hunteria
(Banded Tulip)

3"

Family *Fasciolariidae*

Pleuroploca gigantea
(Florida Horse Conch)

up to 20"

141

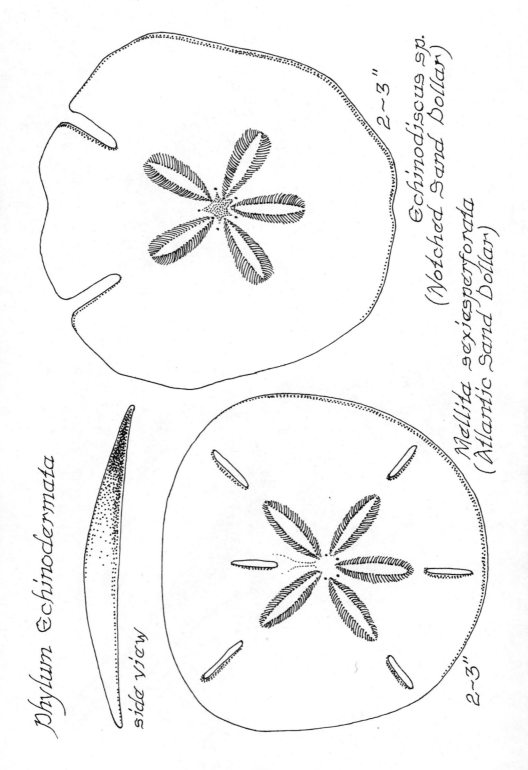

Phylum Echinodermata

side view

Echinodiscus sp.
(Notched Sand Dollar)

2~3"

Mellita sexiesperforata
(Atlantic Sand Dollar)

2~3"

Phylum Echinodermata

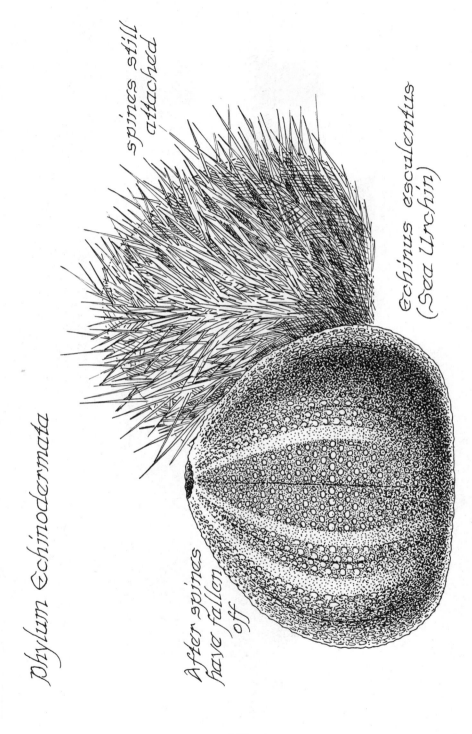

spines still
attached

Echinus esculentus
(Sea Urchin)

After spines
have fallen
off

143

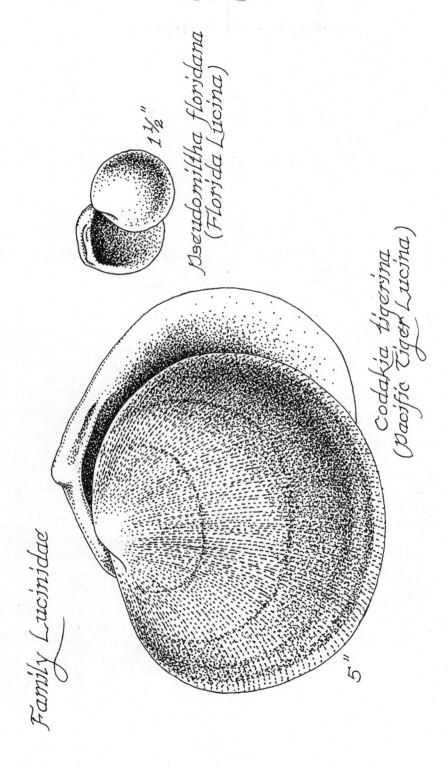

Family Lucinidae

Pseudomiltha floridana
(Florida Lucina)

1½"

Codakia tigerina
(Pacific Tiger Lucina)

5"